W9-BOK-566

The Pursuit of Loneliness

The Pursuit of Loneliness

AMERICAN CULTURE
AT THE BREAKING POINT

Philip E. Slater

BEACON PRESS *BOSTON*

Copyright © 1970 by Philip E. Slater
Library of Congress catalog card number: 79–101327
Standard Book Number: 8070–4180–7
Published simultaneously in Canada by Saunders of Toronto, Ltd.
Beacon Press books are published under the auspices
of the Unitarian Universalist Association
Printed in the United States of America
Third Printing, October 1970

To Wendy, Scott, Stephanie, and Dashka

"Kathy, I'm lost," I said,
Though I knew she was sleeping.
"I'm empty and aching and
I don't know why."
Counting the cars
On the New Jersey Turnpike.
They've all come
To look for America.
PAUL SIMON

Contents

Preface

Once upon a time there was a man who sought escape from the prattle of his neighbors and went to live alone in a hut he had found in the forest. At first he was content, but a bitter winter led him to cut down the trees around his hut for firewood. The next summer he was hot and uncomfortable because his hut had no shade, and he complained bitterly of the harshness of the elements.

He made a little garden and kept some chickens, but rabbits were attracted by the food in the garden and ate much of it. The man went into the forest and trapped a fox, which he tamed and taught to catch rabbits. But the fox ate up the man's chickens as well. The man shot the fox and cursed the perfidy of the creatures of the wild.

The man always threw his refuse on the floor of his hut and soon it swarmed with vermin. He then built an ingenious system of hooks and pulleys so that everything in the hut could be suspended from the ceiling. But the strain was too much for the flimsy hut and it soon collapsed. The man grumbled about the inferior construction of the hut and built himself a new one.

One day he boasted to a relative in his old village about the peaceful beauty and plentiful game surrounding his forest home. The relative was impressed and reported back to his neighbors, who began to use the area for picnics and hunting excursions. The man was upset by this and cursed the intrusiveness of mankind. He began posting signs, setting traps, and shooting at those who came near his dwelling. In revenge groups of boys would come at night from time to time to frighten him and steal things. The man took to sleeping every night in a chair by the window with a loaded shotgun across his knees. One night he turned in his sleep and shot off his foot. The villagers were chastened and saddened by this misfortune and thereafter stayed away from his part of the forest. The man became lonely and cursed the unfriendliness and indifference of his former neighbors. And in all this the man saw no agency except what lay outside himself, for which reason, and because of his ingenuity, the villagers called him the American.

My purpose in writing this book is to reach some understanding of the social and psychological forces that are pulling our society apart. I want to talk not about what happens to people but about what people do—to themselves, to each other. Hence I am writing primarily for those people whose behavior has the greatest impact on the society, and who have the power and resources to improve it. Most of what I have to say is about middle-class life, which should be kept in mind whenever it begins to sound as if all Americans attend college or own their own homes. Some awkwardness arises, too, from the effort to speak to the concerns and experiences of both middle-aged and younger groups, since what is important to one may seem incomprehensible or irrelevant to the other. Finally, I am writing for and about Americans. This does not mean that the book is relevant only for Americans—the "two cultures" discussed in Chapter V transcend national boundaries. But the problems to which this book is devoted are most fully developed in America, and it is in America that the major battles will be fought.

*   *   *

A traveler returning to his own country after spending some time abroad obtains a fresh vision of it. He still wears his traveler's antennae—a sensitivity to nuances of custom and attitude that helps him to adapt and make his way in strange settings.

Reentering America, one is struck first of all by the grim monotony of American facial expressions—hard, surly, and bitter—and by the aura of deprivation that informs them. One goes abroad forewarned against exploitation by grasping foreigners, but nothing is done to prepare the returning traveler for the fanatical acquisitiveness of his compatriots. It is difficult to become reaccustomed to seeing people already weighted down with possessions acting as if every object they did not own were bread withheld from a hungry mouth.

These perceptions are heightened by the contrast between the sullen faces of real people and the vision of happiness television offers: men and women ecstatically engaged in stereotyped symbols of fun—running through fields, strolling on beaches, dancing and singing. Smiling faces with chronically open mouths express their gratification with the manifold bounties offered by the culture. One begins to feel there is a severe gap between the fantasies Americans live by and the realities they live *in*. Americans know from an early age how they are supposed to look when happy and what they are supposed to do or buy to be happy. But for some reason their fantasies are unrealizable and leave them disappointed and embittered.

The traveler's antennae disappear after a time. These impressions fade, and the reentry process is gradually effected. America once again seems familiar, comfortable, ordinary. Yet some uneasiness lingers on, for the society seems troubled and self-preoccupied—as if suddenly large numbers of Americans were scrutinizing their own society with the doubtful eyes of a traveler.

PHILIP E. SLATER

The Pursuit of Loneliness

1

I only work here

It's getting hard to be someone,
But it all works out,
It doesn't matter much to me.
LENNON AND MC CARTNEY

All the lonely people—
Where do they all come from?
LENNON AND MC CARTNEY

He said his name was Columbus,
And I just said,"good luck."
DYLAN

One of the functions of a society is to make its inhabitants feel safe, and Americans devote more of their collective resources to security than to any other need. Yet Americans do not feel safe, despite (or because of) shotguns in the closet and nuclear bombers patrolling overhead. With each decade we seem to accumulate more fears, and most of these fears seem to be about each other. In the fifties we were afraid of native Communists, and although we now feel sheepish about *that* moment of panic we express today the same kinds of fear toward blacks, hippies, and student radicals; and in our reactions to all of these fears we have created some very real dangers.

The contrast between our intense fear of small and comparatively unarmed minorities and the Dawn Patrol bravado with which we respond to serious threats of total extinction is rather striking. During the Cuban missile crisis, for example, people interviewed on the street combined a clear awareness that "this may be World War III" with the kind of cheery blandness that psychiatrists label "schizoid" and "inappropriate" when it occurs in a personal context. Given this lack of concern for an overwhelming threat, how can we account for the exaggerated fear of domestic minorities?

From Freud we learned long ago to suspect, when a fear seems out of proportion, that it has been bloated by a wish; and this seems particularly likely when the danger is defined as a psychological one—an evil influence. We fear storms and wild beasts, but we do not censor them. If we must guard ourselves against evil influences we thereby admit their seductive appeal. Thus the McCarthy era reached its peak after the discovery that a few Americans had responded to Chinese "brainwashing" efforts, and the fear of conversion to Communism was quite explicit in public statements and popular surveys. One survey respondent, for example, made the revealing statement that "so many people in America *are eager* like those soldiers of ours in Korea to fall into the trap set by Communist propaganda."[1] The anticommunism of that period and its institutional residues have served as a kind of political fig leaf.

The same emphasis surrounds our fears of radicalism today. Draft resistance, peace demonstrations, black militance, hippie communes, and student protest are disturbing not because they provide a serious physical danger (equivalent to, say, driving a car), but because we fear having our secret doubts about the viability of our social system voiced aloud. It is not what happens abroad that generates hysteria, but rather what appears to be happening within ourselves. This is why force must be used against the expression of certain ideas—if the ideas pluck a responsive chord counterarguments are difficult to remember, and one must fall back on clubs and tear gas.

But what is the nature of the attraction exerted by radical ideas on unwilling conservatives? We know something about the hopes that tinge the old maid's search for a ravisher under her bed, but we need to understand better the seductive impact that informs our enraged fascination with the revolutionary currents of American society. Since the very form of this question rests on certain assumptions about culture and personality, however, let me first make these explicit.

The emotional repertory of human beings is limited and standard. We are built to feel warm, happy, and contented when caressed, to feel angry when frustrated, frightened when attacked, offended when insulted, jealous when excluded, and so on. But every culture holds some of these human reactions to be unacceptable and attempts to warp its participants into some peculiar specialization. Since human beings are malleable within limits, the warping is for the most part successfully achieved, so that some learn not to laugh, some not to cry, some not to love, and some not to hate in situations in which these reactions might appropriately be expressed.

This cultural warping of human emotionality is eased by compartmentalization: there are special times and places and situations where the disparaged responses are permitted, or classes of people who can provide vicarious satisfaction through a conspicuous performance of some kind.

Yet there are always a few of these responses with which every society and every individual has trouble. They must be shouted down continually, although they are usually visible to the outsider. Thus although the Germans, for example, have always placed great stress on order, precision, and obedience to authority, they periodically explode into revolutionary chaos and are driven by romantic Gotterdammerung fantasies. In the same way there is a cooperative underside to competitive America, a rich spoofing tradition in ceremonious England, an elaborated pornography in all prudish societies, and so on. Rather than saying Germans are obedient or Anglo-Saxon societies stuffy or puritanical, it is more correct to say that Germans are preoccupied with issues of authority, Anglo-Saxons with the control of emotional and sexual expression, and so forth. Those issues about which members of a given society seem to feel strongly all reveal a conflict one side of which is strongly emphasized, the other side as strongly (but not quite successfully) suppressed.*

* This kind of thing has been a great boon to literary criticism and biography over the years. Generations of humanists have excited themselves and their readers by showing "contradictions" and "paradoxes" in some real or fictional person's character, simply because a trait and its opposite

These opposing forces are much more equally balanced than the society's participants like to recognize—were this not true there would be no need for suppression. Life would indeed be much less frantic if we were all able to recognize the diversity of responses and feelings within ourselves, and could abandon our somewhat futile efforts to present a monolithic self-portrait to the world. Probably some exaggeration of uniformity is necessary, however, in order for us to act at all, or at least with enough consistency to permit smooth social functioning.

On the individual level the delicate balance reveals itself through conversion. An individual who "converts" from one orientation to its exact opposite appears to himself and others to have made a gross change, but actually it involves only a very small shift in the balance of a focal and persistent conflict. Just as only one percent of the voting population is needed to reverse the results of an American election, so only one percent of an individual's internal "constituencies" need shift in order to transform him from voluptuary to ascetic, from policeman to criminal, from Communist to anticommunist, or whatever. The opposite sides are as evenly matched as before, and the apparent change merely represents the desperate efforts made by the internal "majority" to consolidate its shaky position of dominance. The individual must expend just as much energy shouting down the new "minority" as he did the old; some of the most dedicated witch hunters of the 1950's, for example, were ex-Communists.

On the societal level there are more outlets for the expression of "minority" themes and sentiments, and reversals of emphasis involve more overlap between the opposing trends. The United States, for example, traditionally one of the most prudish societies in the world, has also long displayed, in a somewhat warped and mechanical way, the greatest profusion of sexual stimuli.

These considerations suggest that the fear of radical movements in America derives much of its intensity from the attraction that

---

coexisted in the same person. But in fact traits and their opposites always coexist if the traits are of any intensity, and the whole tradition of cleverly ferreting out paradoxes of character depends upon the psychological naïveté of the reader for its impact. Inadequate psychologies have always been good for business in the academic world.

such movements have for their opponents—an attraction that must be stifled. But what is it? What is so severely lacking in our society that the assertion of an alternative life style throws so many Americans into panic and rage?

I would like to suggest three human desires that are deeply and uniquely frustrated by American culture:

(1) The desire for *community*—the wish to live in trust and fraternal cooperation with one's fellows in a total and visible collective entity.

(2) The desire for *engagement*—the wish to come directly to grips with social and interpersonal problems and to confront on equal terms an environment which is not composed of ego-extensions.

(3) The desire for *dependence*—the wish to share responsibility for the control of one's impulses and the direction of one's life.

When I say that these three desires are frustrated by American culture, this need not conjure up romantic images of the individual struggling against society. In every case it is fair to say that we participate eagerly in producing the frustration we endure—it is not something merely done to us. For these desires are in each case subordinate to their opposites in that vague entity called the American Character. The thesis of this chapter is that Americans have voluntarily created and voluntarily maintain a society which increasingly frustrates and aggravates these secondary yearnings, to the point where they threaten to become primary. Groups that in any way personify this threat are therefore feared in an exaggerated way, and will be until Americans as a group are able to recognize and accept those needs within themselves.

I. COMMUNITY AND COMPETITION

We are so accustomed to living in a society that stresses individualism that we need to be reminded that "collectivism" in a broad sense has always been the more usual lot of mankind, as well as of most other species. Most people in most societies have been born into and died in stable communities in which the subordination of the individual to the welfare of the group was taken for granted, while the aggrandizement of the individual at the expense of his fellows was simply a crime.

This is not to say that competition is an American invention—all societies involve some sort of admixture of cooperative and competitive institutions. But our society lies near or on the competitive extreme, and although it contains cooperative institutions I think it is fair to say that Americans suffer from their relative weakness and peripherality. Studies of business executives have revealed, for example, a deep hunger for an atmosphere of trust and fraternity with their colleagues (with whom they must, in the short run, engage in what Riesman calls "antagonistic cooperation"). The competitive life is a lonely one, and its satisfactions are very short-lived indeed, for each race leads only to a new one.

In the past, as so many have pointed out, there were in our society many oases in which one could take refuge from the frenzied invidiousness of our economic system—institutions such as the extended family and the stable local neighborhood in which one could take pleasure from something other than winning a symbolic victory over one of his fellows. But these have disappeared one by one, leaving the individual more and more in a situation in which he must try to satisfy his affiliative and invidious needs in the same place. This has made the balance a more brittle one—the appeal of cooperative living more seductive, and the need to suppress our longing for it more acute.

In recent decades the principal vehicle for the tolerated expression of this longing has been the mass media. Popular songs and film comedies have continually engaged in a sentimental rejection of the dominant mores, maintaining that the best things in life are free, that love is more important than success, that keeping up with the Joneses is absurd, that personal integrity should take precedence over winning, and so on. But these protestations must be understood for what they are: a safety valve for the dissatisfactions that the modal American experiences when he behaves as he thinks he should. The same man who chuckles and sentimentalizes over a happy-go-lucky hero in a film would view his real-life counterpart as frivolous and irresponsible, and suburbanites who philosophize over their back fence with complete sincerity about their "dog-eat-dog-world," and what-is-it-all-for, and you-can't-take-it-with-you, and success-doesn't-make-you-happy-it-just-gives-you-ulcers-and-a-heart-condition—would be enraged should their children pay serious attention to such a viewpoint. Indeed, the degree of rage is, up to a point, a function of the degree of sincerity: if the individual did not feel these things he would not have to fight them so vigorously. The peculiarly exaggerated hostility that hippies tend to arouse suggests that the life they strive for is highly seductive to middle-aged Americans.

The intensity of this reaction can in part be attributed to a kind of circularity that characterizes American individualism. When a value is as strongly held as is individualism in America the illnesses it produces tend to be treated by increasing the dosage, in the same way an alcoholic treats a hangover or a drug addict his withdrawal symptoms. Technological change, mobility, and the individualistic ethos combine to rupture the bonds that tie each individual to a family, a community, a kinship network, a geographical location—bonds that give him a comfortable sense of himself. As this sense of himself erodes, he seeks ways of affirming it. But his efforts at self-enhancement automatically accelerate the very erosion he seeks to halt.

It is easy to produce examples of the many ways in which Americans attempt to minimize, circumvent, or deny the interdependence upon which all human societies are based. We seek a private house, a private means of transportation, a private garden, a private laundry, self-service stores, and do-it-yourself skills of every kind. An enormous technology seems to have set itself the task of making it unnecessary for one human being ever to ask anything of another in the course of going about his daily business. Even within the family Americans are unique in their feeling that each member should have a separate room, and even a separate telephone, television, and car, when economically possible. We seek more and more privacy, and feel more and more alienated and lonely when we get it. What accidental contacts we do have, furthermore, seem more intrusive, not only because they are unsought but because they are unconnected with any familiar pattern of interdependence.

Most important, our encounters with others tend increasingly to be competitive as a result of the search for privacy. We less and less often meet our fellow man to share and exchange, and more and more often encounter him as an impediment or a nuisance: making the highway crowded when we are rushing somewhere, cluttering and littering the beach or park or wood, pushing in front of us at the supermarket, taking the last parking place, polluting our air and water, building a highway through our house, blocking our view, and so on. Because we have cut off so much communication with each other we keep bumping into each other, and thus a higher and higher percentage of our interpersonal contacts are abrasive.

We seem unable to foresee that the gratification of a wish might turn out to be something of a monkey's paw if the wish were shared by many others. We cheer the new road that initially shaves ten minutes off the drive to our country retreat but ultimately transforms it into a crowded resort and increases both the traffic and the time. We are continually surprised to find, when we want something, that thousands or millions of others want it, too—that other human beings get hot in summer and cold in winter. The worst traffic jams occur when a mass of vacationing tourists departs for home early to "beat the traffic." We are too enamored of the individualistic fantasy that everyone is, or should be, different— that each person could somehow build his entire life around some single, unique eccentricity without boring himself and everyone else to death. Each of us of course has his quirks, which provide a surface variety that is briefly entertaining, but aside from this human beings have little basis for their persistent claim that they are not all members of the same species.

Since our contacts with others are increasingly competitive, unanticipated, and abrasive, we seek still more apartness and accelerate the trend. The desire to be somehow special inaugurates an even more competitive quest for progressively more rare and expensive symbols—a quest that is ultimately futile since it is individualism itself that produces uniformity.

This is poorly understood by Americans, who tend to confuse uniformity with "conformity," in the sense of compliance with or submission to group demands. Many societies exert far more pressure on the individual to mold himself to fit a particularized segment of a total group pattern, but there is variation among these circumscribed roles. Our society gives far more leeway to the individual to pursue his own ends, but, since *it* defines what is worthy and desirable, everyone tends, independently but monotonously, to pursue the same things in the same way. The first pattern combines cooperation, conformity, and variety; the second, competition, individualism, and uniformity.

These relationships are exemplified by two familiar processes in contemporary America: the flight to the suburb and the do-it-yourself movement. Both attempt to deny human interdependence and pursue unrealistic fantasies of self-sufficiency. The first tries to overlook our dependence upon the city for the maintenance of the level of culture we demand. "Civilized" means, literally, "citified," and the state of the city is an accurate index of the condition of the culture as a whole. We behave toward our cities like an irascible farmer who never feeds his cow and then kicks her when she fails to give enough milk. But the flight to the suburb is in any case self-defeating, its goals subverted by the mass quality of the exodus. The suburban dweller seeks peace, privacy, nature, community, and a child-rearing environment which is healthy and culturally optimal. Instead he finds neither the beauty and serenity of the countryside, the stimulation of the city, nor the stability and sense of community of the small town, and his children are exposed to a cultural deprivation equaling that of any slum child with a television set. Living in a narrow age-graded and class-segregated society, it is little wonder that suburban families have contributed so little to the national talent pool in proportion to their numbers, wealth, and other social advantages.* And this transplantation, which has caused the transplants to atrophy, has blighted the countryside and impoverished the city. A final irony of the suburban dream is that, for many Americans, reaching the pinnacle of one's social ambi-

---

* Using cities, small towns, and rural areas for comparison. The small Midwestern town achieves its legendary dullness by a process akin to evaporation—all the warm and energetic particles depart for coastal cities, leaving their place of origin colder and flatter than they found it. But the restless spirit in a small town knows he lives in the sticks and has a limited range of experience, while his suburban counterpart can sustain an illusion of cosmopolitanism in an environment which is far more constricted (a small town is a microcosm, a suburb merely a layer).

tions (owning a house in the suburbs) requires one to perform all kinds of menial tasks (carrying garbage cans, mowing lawns, shoveling snow, and so on) that were performed for him when he occupied a less exalted status.

Some of this manual labor, however, is voluntary—an attempt to deny the elaborate division of labor required in a complex society. Many Americans seem quite willing to pay this price for their reluctance to engage in interpersonal encounters with servants and artisans—a price which is rather high unless the householder particularly relishes the work (some find in it a tangible relief from the intangibles they manipulate in their own jobs) or is especially good at it, or cannot command a higher rate of pay in the job market than the servant or artisan.

The do-it-yourself movement has accompanied, paradoxically, increasing specialization in the occupational sphere. As one's job narrows, perhaps, one seeks the challenge of new skill-acquisition in the home. But specialization also means that one's interpersonal encounters with artisans in the home proliferate and become more impersonal. It is not a matter of a familiar encounter with the local smith or grocer—a few well-known individuals performing a relatively large number of functions, and with whom one's casual interpersonal contacts may be a source of satisfaction, and are in any case a testimony to the stability and meaningful interrelatedness of human affairs. One finds instead a multiplicity of narrow specialists —each perhaps a stranger (the same type of repair may be performed by a different person each time). Every relationship, such as it is, must start from scratch, and it is small wonder that the householder turns away from such an unrewarding prospect in apathy and despair.

Americans thus find themselves in a vicious circle, in which their extrafamilial relationships are increasingly arduous, competitive, trivial, and irksome, in part as a result of efforts to avoid or minimize potentially irksome or competitive relationships. As the few vestiges of stable and familiar community life erode, the desire for a simple, cooperative life style grows in intensity. The most seductive appeal of radical ideologies for Americans consists in the fact that all in one way or another attack the competitive foundations of our society. Each touches a responsive doubt, and the stimuli arousing this doubt must be carefully unearthed and rooted out, just as the Puritan must unearth and root out the sexual stimuli that excite him.*

Now it may be objected that American society is far less competitive than it once was, and the appeal of radical ideologies should hence be diminished. A generation of critics has argued that the entrepreneurial individualist of the past has been replaced by a bureaucratic, security-minded, Organization Man. Much of this historical drama was written through the simple device of comparing yesterday's owner-president with today's assistant sales manager; certainly these nostalgia-merchants never visited a nineteenth-century company town. Another distortion is introduced by the fact that it was only the most ruthlessly competitive robber barons who survived to tell us how it was. Little is written about the neighborhood store that extended credit to the poor, or the small town industry that refused to lay off local workers in hard times—they all went under together. And as for the organization men—they left us no sagas.

Despite these biases real changes have undoubtedly occurred, but even if we grant that the business world as such was more competitive, the total environment contained more cooperative, stable, and personal elements. The individual worked in a smaller firm with lower turnover in which his relationships were more enduring and less impersonal, and in which the ideology of Adam Smith was tempered by the fact that the participants were neighbors and might have been childhood playmates. Even if the business world was as "dog-eat-dog" as we imagine it (which seems highly unlikely), one encountered it as a deviant episode in what was otherwise a more comfortable and familiar environment than the organization man can find today in or out of his office. The or-

* Both efforts are ambivalent, since the "seek and destroy" process is in part a quest for the stimulus itself. The Puritanical censor both wants the sexual stimulus and wants to destroy it, and his job enables him to gratify both of these "contradictory" desires. There is a similar prurience in the efforts of groups such as the House UnAmerican Activities Committee to "uncover subversion." Just as the censor gets to experience far more pornography than the average man, so the Congressional red-baiter gets to hear as much Communist ideology as he wants, which is apparently quite a lot.

ganization man complex is simply an attempt to restore the personal, particularistic, paternalistic environment of the family business and the company town; and the other-directed "group-think" of the suburban community is a desperate attempt to bring some old-fashioned small-town collectivism into the transient and impersonal life-style of the suburb. The social critics of the 1950's were so preoccupied with assailing these rather synthetic substitutes for traditional forms of human interdependence that they lost sight of the underlying pathogenic forces that produced them. Medical symptoms usually result from attempts made by the body to counteract disease, and attacking such symptoms often aggravates and prolongs the illness. This appears to be the case with the feeble and self-defeating efforts of twentieth-century Americans to find themselves a viable social context.

II. ENGAGEMENT AND UNINVOLVEMENT

Many of the phenomena we have discussed can also be linked to a compulsive American tendency to avoid confrontation of chronic social problems. This avoiding tendency often comes as a surprise to foreigners, who tend to think of Americans as pragmatic and down-to-earth. But while trying to solve long-range social problems with short-run "hardware" solutions produces a lot of hardware—a down-to-earth result, surely—it can hardly be considered practical when it aggravates the problems, as it almost always does. American pragmatism is deeply irrational in this respect, and in our hearts we have always known it. One of the favorite themes of American cartoonists is the man who paints himself into a corner, saws off the limb he is sitting on, or runs out of space on the sign he is printing. The scientist of science-fiction and horror films, whose experimentation leads to disastrously unforeseen consequences, is a more anxious representation of this same awareness that the most future-oriented nation in the world shows a deep incapacity to plan ahead. We are, as a people, perturbed by our inability to anticipate the consequences of our acts, but we still wait optimistically for some magic telegram, informing us that the tangled skein of misery and self-deception into which we have woven ourselves has vanished in the night. Each month popular magazines regale their readers with such telegrams: announcing that our transportation crisis will be solved by a bigger plane or a wider road, mental illness with a pill, poverty with a law, slums with a bulldozer, urban conflict with a gas, racism with a goodwill gesture. Perhaps the most grotesque of all these telegrams was an article in *Life* showing a group of sub-urbanites participating in a "Clean-Up Day" in an urban slum. Foreigners are surprised when Americans exhibit this kind of naïveté and/or cynicism about social problems, but their surprise is inappropriate. Whatever realism we may display in technical areas, our approach to social issues inevitably falls back on cinematic tradition, in which social problems are resolved by gesture. Deeply embedded in the somnolent social consciousness of the broom-wielding suburbanites is a series of climactic movie scenes in which a long column of once surly natives, marching in solemn silence and as one man, framed by the setting sun, turn in their weapons to the white chief who has done them a good turn, or menace the white adventurer's enemy (who turns pale at the sight), or rebuild the missionary's church, destroyed by fire.

When a social problem persists (as they tend to do) longer than a few days, those who call attention to its continued presence are viewed as "going too far" and "causing the pendulum to swing the other way." We can make war on poverty but shrink from the extensive readjustments required to stop breeding it. Once a law is passed, a commission set up, a study made, a report written, the problem is expected to have been "wiped out" or "mopped up." Bombs abroad are matched by "crash programs" at home—the terminological similarity reveals a psychological one. Our approach to transportation problems has had the effect, as many people have observed, of making it easier and easier to travel to more and more places that have become less and less worth driving to. Asking us to consider the manifold consequences of chopping down a for-est, draining a swamp, spraying a field with poison, making it easier to drive into an already crowded city, or selling deadly weapons to everyone who wants them arouses in us the same im-patience as a chess problem would in a hyperactive six-year-old.

The avoiding tendency lies at the very root of American charac-ter. This nation was settled and continuously repopulated by peo-ple who were not personally successful in confronting the social conditions obtaining in their mother country, but fled these conditions in the hope of a better life. This series of choices (reproduced in the westward movement) provided a complex selection process —populating America disproportionately with a certain kind of person.

In the past we have always, explicitly or implicitly, stressed the positive side of this selection, implying that America thereby found itself blessed with an unusual number of energetic, mobile, ambitious, daring, and optimistic persons. Now there is no reason to deny that a number of traits must have helped to differentiate those who chose to come from those who chose to stay, nor that these differences must have generated social institutions and habits of mind that tended to preserve and reproduce these characteristics. But very little attention has been paid to the more negative aspects of the selection. If we gained the energetic and daring we also gained the lion's share of the rootless, the unscrupulous, those who value money over relationships, and those who put self-aggrandizement ahead of love and loyalty. And most of all, we gained a critically undue proportion of persons who, when faced with a difficult situation, tended to chuck the whole thing and flee to a new environment. Escaping, evading, and avoiding are responses which lie at the base of much that is peculiarly American—the suburb, the automobile, the self-service store, and so on.

These responses also contribute to the appalling discrepancy between our material resources and our treatment of those who cannot adequately care for themselves. This is not an argument against institutionalization: American society is not geared to handle these problems in any other way, and this is in fact the point I wish to make. One cannot successfully alter one facet of a social system if everything else is left the same, for the patterns are interdependent and reinforce one another. In a cooperative, stable society the aged, infirm, or psychotic person can be absorbed by the local community, which knows and understands him. He presents a difficulty which is familiar and which can be confronted daily and directly. This condition cannot be reproduced in our society today—the burden must be carried by a small, isolated, mobile family unit that is not really equipped for it.

But understanding the forces that require us to incarcerate those who cannot function independently in our society does not give us license to ignore the significance of doing so. The institutions we provide for those who cannot care for themselves are human garbage heaps—they result from and reinforce our tendency to avoid confronting social and interpersonal problems. They make life "easier" for the rest of society, just as does the automobile. And just as we find ourselves having to devise ridiculous exercises to counteract the harmful effects of our dependence upon the automobile, so the "ease" of our nonconfronting social technology makes us bored, flabby, and interpersonally insensitive, and our lives empty and mechanical.

Our ideas about institutionalizing the aged, psychotic, retarded, and infirm are based on a pattern of thought that we might call the Toilet Assumption—the notion that unwanted matter, unwanted difficulties, unwanted complexities and obstacles will disappear if they are removed from our immediate field of vision. We do not connect the trash we throw from the car window with the trash in our streets, and we assume that replacing old buildings with new expensive ones will alleviate poverty in the slums. We throw the aged and psychotic into institutional holes where they cannot be seen. Our approach to social problems is to decrease their visibility: out of sight, out of mind. This is the real foundation of racial segregation, especially its most extreme case, the Indian "reservation." The result of our social efforts has been to remove the underlying problems of our society farther and farther from daily experience and daily consciousness, and hence to decrease, in the mass of the population, the knowledge, skill, resources, and motivation necessary to deal with them.

When these discarded problems rise to the surface again—a riot, a protest, an exposé in the mass media—we react as if a sewer had backed up. We are shocked, disgusted, and angered, and immediately call for the emergency plumber (the special commission, the crash program) to ensure that the problem is once again removed from consciousness.

The Toilet Assumption is not merely a facetious metaphor. Prior to the widespread use of the flush toilet all of humanity was daily confronted with the immediate reality of human waste and its disposal. They knew where it was and how it got there. Nothing miraculously vanished. Excrement was conspicuously present in the outhouse or chamber pot, and the slops that went out the window went visibly and noticeably into the street. The most aristocratic Victorian ladies strolling in fashionable city parks thought nothing of retiring to the bushes to relieve themselves. Similarly, garbage did not disappear down a disposal unit—it remained nearby.

As with physical waste, so with social problems. The biblical adage, "the poor are always with us," had a more literal meaning before World War I. The poor were visible and all around. Psychosis was not a strange phenomenon in a textbook but a familiar neighbor or village character. The aged were in every house. Everyone had seen animals slaughtered and knew what they were eating when they ate them; illness and death were a part of everyone's immediate experience.

In contemporary life the book of experience is filled with blank and mysterious pages. Occupational specialization and plumbing have exerted a kind of censorship over our understanding of the world we live in and how it operates. And when we come into immediate contact with anything that does not seem to fit into the ordinary pattern of our somewhat bowdlerized existence our spontaneous reaction is to try somehow to flush it away, bomb it away, throw it down the jail.

But in some small degree we also feel bored and uneasy with the orderly chrome and porcelain vacuum of our lives, from which so much of life has been removed. Evasion creates self-distaste as well as comfort, and radical confrontations are exciting as well as disruptive. The answering chord that they produce within us terrifies us, and although we cannot entirely contain our fascination, it is relatively easy to project our self-disgust onto the perpetrators of the confrontations.

This ambivalence is reflected in the mass media. The hunger for confrontation and experience attracts a lot of attention to social problems, but these are usually dealt with in such a way as to reinforce the avoidance process. The TV documentary presents a tidy package with opposing views and an implication of progress. Reports in popular magazines attempt to provide a substitute for actual experience. Important book and film reviews, for example, give just the blend of titillation and condescension to make the reader imagine that he is already "in" and need not undergo the experience itself—that he has not only participated in the novel adventure but already outgrown it. Thus the ultimate effect of the media is to reinforce the avoiding response by providing an effigy of confrontation and experience. There is always the danger with such insulating mechanisms, however, that they at times get overloaded, like tonsils, and become carriers of precisely the agents against which they are directed. This is an increasingly frequent event in our society today.

A corollary of this latent desire for social confrontation is the desire for an incorruptible man—a man who cannot be bribed, who does not have his price. Once again this desire is a recessive trait, relegated largely to the realm of folk drama and movie script, but it exists nonetheless, as a silent rebellion against the oppressive democratic harmony of a universal monetary criterion.

In the hard reality of everyday life, however, the incorruptible man is at best an inconvenience, an obstacle to the smooth functioning of a vast institutional machinery. Management leaders, for example, tend to prefer corrupt union leaders—"people you can do business with"—to those who might introduce questions and attitudes lying outside the rules of a monetary game. The man who cannot be bought tends to be mistrusted as a fanatic, and the fact that incorruptible men are so often called Communists may be understood in the same light. As in the case of the mass media, however, this mechanism has become overloaded, so that having been jailed and/or called a Communist or traitor is now regarded by young adults as a medal attesting to one's social concern.

Also closely related to the latent desire for confrontation is an inarticulate wish to move in an environment consisting of something other than our own creations. Human beings evolved as organisms geared to mastery of the natural environment. Within the past few thousand years we have learned to perform this function so well that the natural environment poses very little threat to civilized peoples. Our dangers are self-made ones—subtle, insidious, and meaningless. We die from our own machines, our own poisons, our own weapons, our own despair. Furthermore, we are separated from primitive conditions by too few millennia to have evolved any comfortable adaptation to a completely man-made environment. We still long for and enjoy struggling against the elements, even though such activity can only occasionally be considered meaningful or functional.* We cross the ocean in artificially primitive boats, climb mountains we could fly over, kill animals we do not eat. Natural disasters, such as floods, hurricanes, blizzards, and so on, generate a cheerfulness which would seem inappropriate if we did not all share it. It is as if some balance between man and nature had been restored, and with it man's "true function." Like the cat that prefers to play with a ball around the obstacle of a chair leg, so man seems to derive some perverse joy from having a snowstorm force him to use the most primitive mode of transportation. It is particularly amusing to observe people following the course of an approaching hurricane and affecting a proper and prudent desire that it veer off somewhere, in the face of an ill-concealed craving that it do nothing of the kind. There is a satisfaction that comes from relating to nature on equal terms, with respect and even deference to forms of life different from ourselves—as the Indian respects the deer he kills for food and the tree that shields him from the sun.

We interact largely with extensions of our own egos. We stumble over the consequences of our past acts. We are drowning in our own excreta (another consequence of the Toilet Assumption). We rarely come into contact with a force which is clearly and cleanly Not-Us. Every struggle is a struggle with ourselves, because there is a little piece of ourselves in everything we encounter—houses, clothes, cars, cities, machines, even our foods. There is an uneasy, anesthetized feeling about this kind of life—like being trapped forever inside an air-conditioned car with power steering and power brakes and only a telephone to talk to. Our world is only a mirror, and our efforts mere shadowboxing—yet shadowboxing in which we frequently manage to hurt ourselves.

* The cholesterol problem provides an illustration: one theory proposes that the release of cholesterol into the bloodstream was functional for hunting large animals with primitive weapons. Since the animal was rarely killed but only wounded, he had to be followed until he dropped, and this was a matter of walking or running for several days without food or rest. A similar response would be activated today in fields such as advertising, in which a sustained extra effort over a period of time (to obtain a large contract, for example) is periodically required. But these peak efforts do not involve any physical release—the cholesterol is not utilized.

Even that part of the world which is not man-made impinges upon us through a symbolic network we have created. We encounter primarily our own fantasies: we have a concept and image of a mountain, a lake, or a forest almost before we ever see one. Travel posters tell us what it means to be in a strange land, the events of life become news items before they actually happen—all experience receives preliminary structure and interpretation. Public relations, television drama, and life become indistinguishable.

The story of Pygmalion is thus the story of modern man, in love with his own product. But like all discreet fairy tales, that of Pygmalion stops with the consummation of his love. It does not tell us of his ineffable boredom at having nothing to love but an excrescence of himself. But we know that men who live surrounded by that which and those whom they have molded to their desires— from the Caliph of Baghdad to Federico Fellini—suffer from a fearsome ennui. The minute they assume material form our fantasies cease to be interesting and become mere excreta.

III. DEPENDENCE AND INDEPENDENCE

Independence training in American society begins almost at birth— babies are held and carried less than in most societies and spend more time in complete isolation—and continues, despite occasional parental ambivalence, throughout childhood and adolescence. When a child is admonished to be a "big boy" or "big girl" this usually means doing something alone or without help (the rest of the time it involves strangling feelings, but this norm seems to be on the wane). Signs of independence are usually rewarded, and a child who in too obvious a manner calls attention to the fact that human intelligence is based almost entirely on the process of imitation is ridiculed by calling him a copycat or a monkey (after the paradoxical habit humans have of projecting their most uniquely human attributes onto animals).

There have been many complaints in recent years that independence training is less rigorous than it once was, but again, as in the case of competitiveness, this is hard to assess. To be on one's own in a simple, stable, and familiar environment requires a good deal less internal "independence" than to be on one's own in a complex, shifting, and strange one. Certainly a child could run about more freely a century ago without coming to harm, and his errors and misdeeds had far more trivial consequences than today; but this decline in the child's freedom of movement says nothing about the degree to which the child is asked to forego the pleasures of depending upon his parents for nurturance and support. If the objective need is greater, it may offset a small increase in parental tolerance for dependent behavior, and cause the child to experience the independence training as more severe rather than less.

In any case, American independence training is severe relative to most of the rest of the world, and we might assume this to have emotional consequences. This is not to say that such training is not consonant with the demands of adult society: the two are quite in accord. Sociologists and anthropologists are often content to stop at this point and say that as long as this accord exists there is no problem worth discussing. But the frustration of any need has its effects (one of them being to increase the society's vulnerability to social change) and these should be understood.

An example might help clarify this issue. Ezra and Suzanne Vogel observe that Japanese parents encourage dependency as actively as American parents push independence, and that healthy children and adults in Japan rely heavily on others for emotional support and decisions about their lives. A degree of dependence on the mother which in America would be considered "abnormal" prepares the Japanese for a society in which far more dependency is expected and accepted than in ours. The Japanese firm is highly paternalistic and takes a great deal of responsibility for making the individual employee secure and comfortable. The Vogels observe, however, that just as the American mother tends to complain at the success of her efforts and feel that her children are *too* independent, so the Japanese mother tends to feel that her children are too *dependent*, despite the fact that she has trained them this way.[2]

What I am trying to point out is that regardless of the congruence between socialization practices and adult norms, any extreme pattern of training will produce stresses for the individuals involved. And just as the mothers experience discomfort with the effects of these patterns, so do the children, although barred by cultural values from recognizing and naming the nature of their distress, which in our society takes the form of a desire to relinquish responsibility for control and decision-making in one's daily life. Deeply felt democratic values usually stand in the way of realizing this goal through authoritarian submission, although our attitudes toward democracy are not without ambivalence, as has been suggested elsewhere;[3] but the temptation to abdicate self-direction in more subtle ways is powerful indeed. Perhaps the major problem for Americans is that of choice: Americans are forced into making more choices per day, with fewer "givens," more ambiguous criteria, less environmental stability, and less social structural support, than any people in history.

Many of the mechanisms through which dependency is counteracted in our society have already been discussed in the preceding sections, but a word should be said about the complex problem of internalized controls. In stable societies, as many authors have pointed out, the control of human impulses is usually a collective responsibility. The individual is viewed as not having within himself the controls required to guarantee that his impulses will not break out in ways disapproved by the community. But this matters very little, since the group is always near at hand to stop him or shame him or punish him should he forget himself.

In more fluid, changing societies we are more apt to find controls that are internalized—that do not depend to so great an extent on control and enforcement by external agents. This has long been characteristic of American society—de Tocqueville observed in 1830 that American women were much more independent than European women, freer from chaperonage, and able to appear in what a European would consider "compromising" situations without any sign of sexual involvement.

Chaperonage is in fact the simplest way to illustrate the difference between external and internalized controls. In chaperon cultures—such as traditional Middle-Eastern and Latin societies—it simply did not occur to anyone that a man and woman could be alone together and not have sexual intercourse. In America, which represents the opposite extreme, there is almost no situation in which a man and a woman could find themselves in which sexual intercourse could not at least be considered problematic (Hollywood comedies have exploited this phenomenon—well past the point of exhaustion and nausea—over the past 35 years). Americans are virtuosi of internalized control of sexual expression (the current relaxation of sexual norms in no way changes this), and this has caused difficulties whenever the two systems have come into contact. An unchaperoned girl in a bikini or mini-skirt means one thing in America, another in Baghdad. It is a mistake to consider a chaperon society more prudish—the compliment is likely to be returned when the difference is understood. Even Americans consider some situations inherently sexual: if a girl from some mythical culture came to an American's house, stripped, and climbed into bed with him, he would assume she was making a sexual overture and would be rather indignant if he found that she was merely expressing casual friendship according to her native customs. He would also be puzzled if *he* were called prudish, and we need not speculate as to what he would call *her*.

But how are internalized controls created? We know that they are closely tied to what are usually called "love-oriented" techniques of discipline in childhood. These techniques avoid physical punishment and deprivation of privileges and stress reasoning and the withdrawal of parental affection. The basic difference between "love-oriented" and "fear-oriented" techniques (such as physical punishment) is that in the latter case the child simply learns to avoid punishment while in the former he tends to incorporate parental values as his own in order to avoid losing parental love and approval. When fear-oriented techniques prevail, the child is in the position of inhabitants of an occupied country, who obey to avoid getting hurt but disobey whenever they think they can get away with it. Like them, the child does not have any emotional commitment to his rulers—he does not fear losing their love.

Love-oriented techniques require by definition that love and discipline emanate from the same source. When this happens it is not merely a question of avoiding the punisher: the child wishes to anticipate the displeasure of the loved and loving parent, wants to be like the parent, and takes into himself as a part of himself the values and attitudes of the parent. He wants to please, not placate, and because he has taken the parent's attitudes as his own, pleasing the parent comes to mean making him feel good about himself. Thus while individuals raised with fear-oriented techniques tend to direct anger outward under stress, those raised with love-oriented techniques tend to direct it inward in the form of guilt—a distinction that has important physiological correlates.[4]

Under stable conditions external controls work perfectly well. Everyone knows his own place and his neighbor's, and deviations from expected behavior will be quickly met from all sides. When social conditions fluctuate, social norms change, and people move frequently from one social setting to another and are often among strangers, this will no longer do. An individual cannot take his whole community with him wherever he goes, and in any case the rules differ from place to place. The mobile individual must travel light, and internalized controls are portable and transistorized, as it were.

Anger directed inward is also made for mobile conditions. In a stable community two youths who start to get into a fight will be held back by their friends—they depend upon this restraint and can abandon themselves to their passion, knowing that it will not produce harmful consequences. But where one moves among strangers it becomes increasingly important to have other mechanisms for handling aggression. In situations of high mobility and flux the individual must have a built-in readiness to feel himself responsible when things go wrong.

Most modern societies are a confused mixture of both systems, a fact that enables conservative spokesmen to attribute rising crime rates to permissive child-rearing techniques. The overwhelmingly majority of ordinary crimes, however, are committed by individuals who have *not* been reared with love-oriented techniques, but, insofar as the parent or parents have been able to rear them at all, by the haphazard use of fear-oriented discipline. Love-oriented child-rearing techniques are a luxury that slum parents, for example, can seldom afford.

Furthermore, it is rather misleading to refer to the heavily guilt-inducing socialization techniques of middle-class parents as "permissive." Misbehavior in a lower class child is more often greeted with a cuff, possibly accompanied by some non-informative response such as "stop that!" But it may not be at all clear to the child which of the many motions he is now performing "that" is; and, indeed, "that" may be punished only when the parent is feeling irritable. A child would have to have achieved an enormously high intelligence level (which, of course, it has not, for this very reason) to be able to form a moral concept out of a hundred irritable stop-thats. What he usually forms is merely a crude sense of when the "old man" or the "old lady" is to be avoided. The self-conscious, highly verbal, middle-class parent is at the opposite extreme. He or she feels that discipline should relate to the child's act, not the parent's own emotional state, and is very careful to emphasize verbally the principle involved in the misbehavior ("it's bad to hit people" or "we have to share with guests"). Concept-formation is made very easy for the middle-class child, and he tends to think of moral questions in terms of principles.

As he grows older this tendency is reinforced by his encounter with different groups with different norms. In a mobile society, one cannot simply accept the absolute validity of any rule because one experiences competing moral codes. As a result the middle-class child tends to evolve a system of meta-rules, that is, rules for assessing the relative validity of these codes. The meta-rules tend to be based upon the earliest and most general principles expressed by the parents; such as prohibitions on violence against others, egalitarianism, mutuality, and so on. This ability to treat rules in a highly secular fashion while maintaining a strong moral position is baffling to those whose control mechanisms are more primitive, but it presupposes a powerful and articulate conscience. Such an individual can expose himself to physical harm and to violence-arousing situations without losing control and while maintaining a moral position. This may seem inconceivable to an uneducated working-class policeman whose own impulses are barely held in line by a jerry-built structure of poorly articulated and mutually contradictory moral absolutes. Hence he tends to misinterpret radical middle-class behavior as a hypocritical mask for mere delinquency.

The point of this long digression, however, is that internalization is a mixed blessing. It may enable one to get his head smashed in a good cause, but the capacity to give oneself up completely to an emotion is almost altogether lost in the process. Where internalization is high there is often a feeling that the controls themselves are out of control—that emotion cannot be expressed when the individual would like to express it. Life is muted, experience filtered, emotion anesthetized, affective discharge incomplete. Efforts to shake free from this hypertrophied control system include not only drugs, and sensation-retrieval techniques such as those developed at the Esalen Institute in California, but also confused attempts to reestablish external systems of direction and control—the vogue currently enjoyed by astrology is an expression of this. The simplest technique, of course, would be the establishment of a more authoritarian social structure, which would relieve the individual of the great burden of examining and moderating his own responses. He could become as a child, lighthearted, spontaneous, and passionate, secure in the knowledge that others would prevent his impulses from causing harm.

Realization of this goal is prevented by democratic values and the social conditions that foster them (complexity, fluidity, change). But the desire plays a significant part in conventional reactions to radical minorities, who are all felt to be seeking the abandonment of self-restraints of one kind or another and at the same time demanding *more* responsible behavior from the establishment. This is both infuriating and contagious to white middle-class adults, who would like very much to do the same, and their call for "law and order" (that is, more *external* control) is an expression of that desire as well as an attempt to smother it. This conflict over dependency and internalization also helps explain why official American anticommunism always lays so much stress on the authoritarian (rather than the socialistic) aspects of Communist states.

INDIVIDUALISM REASSESSED

The three variables we have been discussing—community, engagement, dependency—can all trace their suppression in American society to our commitment to individualism. The belief that everyone should pursue autonomously his own destiny has forced us to maintain an emotional detachment (for which no amount of superficial gregariousness can compensate) from our social and physical environment, and aroused a vague guilt about our competitiveness and indifference to others; for, after all, our earliest training in childhood does not stress competitiveness, but cooperation, sharing, and thoughtfulness—it is only later that we learn to reverse these priorities. Radical challenges to our society, then, always tap a confused responsive chord within us that is far more disturbing than anything going on outside. They threaten to reconnect us with each other, with nature, and with ourselves, a possibility that is thrilling but terrifying—as if we had grown a shell-like epidermis and someone was threatening to rip it off.

Individualism finds its roots in the attempt to deny the reality and importance of human interdependence. One of the major goals of technology in America is to "free" us from the necessity of relating to, submitting to, depending upon, or controlling other people.* Unfortunately, the more we have succeeded in doing this the more we have felt disconnected, bored, lonely, unprotected, unnecessary, and unsafe.

Individualism has many expressions: free enterprise, self-service, academic freedom, suburbia, permissive gun-laws, civil liberties, do-it-yourself, oil-depletion allowances. Everyone values some of these expressions and condemns others, but the principle is widely shared. Criticisms of our society since World War II have almost all embraced this value and expressed fears for its demise—the organization man, the other-directed man, conformity, "group-think," and so on. In general these critics have failed to see the role of the value they embrace so fervently in generating the phenomena they so detest.

The most sophisticated apologist for individualism is David Riesman, who recognizes at least that uniformity and community are not the same thing, and does not shrink from the insoluble dilemmas that these issues create. Perhaps the definitive and revealing statement of what individualism is all about is his: "I am insisting

---

* The peculiar germ-phobia that pervades American life (and supports several industries) owes much to this insulation machinery. So far have we carried the fantasy of individual autonomy that we imagine each person to have his own unique species of germs, which must therefore not be mixed and confused with someone else's. We are even disturbed at the presence of the germs themselves: despite the fact that many millions of them inhabit every healthy human body from the cradle to the grave we regard them as trespassers. We feel that nature has no business claiming a connection with us, and perhaps one day we will prove ourselves correct.

that no ideology, however noble, can justify the sacrifice of an individual to the needs of the group."[5]

Whenever I hear such sentiments I recall Jay Haley's discussion of the kind of communication that characterizes the families of schizophrenics. He points out that people who communicate with one another necessarily govern each other's behavior—set rules for each other. But an individual may attempt to avoid this human fate —to become independent, uninvolved: ". . . he may choose the schizophrenic way and indicate that nothing he does is done in relationship to other people." The family of the schizophrenic establishes a system of rules like all families, but also has "a prohibition on any acknowledgement that a family member is setting rules. Each refuses to concede that he is circumscribing the behavior of others, and each refuses to concede that any other family member is governing him." The attempt, of course, fails. "The more a person tries to avoid being governed or governing others, the more helpless he becomes and so governs others by forcing them to take care of him."[6] In our society as a whole this caretaking role is assigned to technology, like so much else.

Riesman overlooks the fact that the individual is sacrificed either way. If he is never sacrificed to the group the group will collapse and the individual with it. Part of the individual is, after all, committed to the group. Part of him wants what "the group" wants, part does not. No matter what is done some aspect of the individual —id, ego, or whatever—will be sacrificed.

An individual, like a group, is a motley collection of ambivalent feelings, contradictory needs and values, and antithetical ideas. He is not, and cannot be, a monolithic totality, and the modern effort to bring this myth to life is not only delusional and ridiculous, but also acutely destructive, both to the individual and to his society.

Recognition of this internal complexity would go a long way toward resolving the dilemma Riesman implicitly poses. For the reason a group needs the kind of creative deviant Riesman values is the same reason it needs to sacrifice him: the failure of the group members to recognize the complexity and diversity and ambivalence within themselves. Since they have oversimplified and rejected parts of themselves, they not only lack certain resources but also are unable to tolerate their naked exposure by others. The deviant is a compensatory mechanism to mitigate this condition. He comes along and tries to provide what is "lacking" in the group (that is, what is present but denied, suppressed). His role is like that of the mutant—most are sacrificed but a few survive to save the group from itself in times of change. Individualism is a kind of desperate plea to save all mutants, on the grounds that we do not know what we are or what we need. As such it is horribly expensive—a little like setting a million chimps to banging on a typewriter on the grounds that eventually one will produce a masterpiece.

But if we abandon the monolithic pretense and recognize that any group sentiment, and its opposite, represents a part of everyone but only a part, then the prophet is unnecessary since he exists in all of us. And should he appear it will be unnecessary to sacrifice him since we have already admitted that what he is saying is true. And in the meantime we would be able to exercise our humanity, governing each other and being governed, instead of encasing ourselves in the leaden armor of our technological schizophrenia.

2

Kill anything that moves

*I am afeard there are few die well that die in a battle;
for how can they charitably dispose of any thing, when
blood is their argument?*
SHAKESPEARE

*Am I a spy in the land of the living,
That I should deliver men to Death?*
MILLAY

*The whole wide human race is taking far too much
methedrine.*
LEITCH

The past few years in America have seen the gradual disintegration
of the illusion that we are not a violent people. Americans have
always admitted being lawless relative to Europeans, but this was
explained as a consequence of our youth as a nation—our closeness
to frontier days. High crime rates prior to World War II were
regarded in much the same manner as the escapades of an active
ten-year-old ("America is all boy!"), and a secret contempt suf-
fused our respect for the law-abiding English. Today the chuckle
is gone, the respect more genuine, for the casual violence of American life has become less casual, and its victims threaten to include
those other than the disadvantaged.

It must be remembered that law and order is an experience the
black American has never had. Lynchings did not "disturb the
peace" so long as you were white. And although Northerners
looked askance at the practice, these were, after all, remote events.

29

But even in the North a black man has never been able to walk down any street he wished without risking arrest, insults, and even beatings from police. There are few even middle-class blacks who have not experienced arrest or the threat of it merely by virtue of having been in the wrong location at the wrong time of day or too casually dressed. Whites are now beginning to experience a comparable problem: the inability to move in certain areas of the city at certain times without the threat of violence. The demand for "law and order" then, is a demand for a return to the days when the more advantaged groups in our society held a monopoly on this scarce commodity.

This exemplifies the difficulty of evaluating changes in the level of domestic violence. So long as the society was decentralized the chronic violence in city slums and certain rural areas did not disturb the society as a whole. But the mass media have flooded out local boundaries and forced the total society into a dim awareness of what it is like to live in fear. It is not so much the increase in violence that upsets middle-class Americans as the democratization of violence: the poor and black have become less willing to serve as specialized victims of violence from whites ("legally") and each other (illegally).

The same point can be made about crimes against property, given the well-known class bias in our legal system. Since the ways in which the rich steal from the poor are rarely defined as crimes (when executives of a major corporation were jailed for a few days some years ago for stealing millions of dollars from the public through antitrust violations many people were shocked that respectable men could be treated in such a rude fashion) rising property-crime rates may only reflect an increase in the democratization of larceny, a result attributable in part to the success of the mass media in convincing the poor that only the possession of various products can satisfy their various social, sexual, and moral requirements.

Leaving aside these more subtle considerations, nonlegal activities of all kinds are far more likely to be considered violent when they have political overtones. Our nation has never known a time without serious urban riots—usually racial or ethnic in origin—but it was only when they began to have a political thrust and to attack white economic exploitation that the concern about rioting began to grow.

The same relationship holds for the college campus. It is not violence as such but its political aims that arouse concern. The same men who assail the violence of campus radicals are quite happy to regale listeners with tales of their own (apolitical) boyhood pranks —pranks that would bring a jail sentence if committed today. College students on many campuses have rioted annually for generations, and the injuries and vandalism resulting from such riots have often far exceeded that produced by protests. Yet these apolitical riots have always been considered venial. The difference is that student pranks and riots in the past attacked authority but accepted it. The protests of today confront authority and question it. Thus although no violence at all may occur, those toward whom the protest is directed may feel that violence has been done to them. The disruption of ordinary daily patterns and assumptions is experienced as a kind of psychological violence.

Consider what happens when a defective traffic light fails to change from red to green. The line of cars grows and restlessness increases. At some point someone decides that the symbol of order is in fact in disorder and either goes through the red light or begins to honk his horn. As soon as one goes through, the others all follow suit. The initiator in this situation is engaging in a kind of civil disobedience. He is challenging the specific rule about red lights in terms of a broader understanding which says that the purpose of traffic laws is to regulate traffic not to disrupt it. Yet because the situation has no real political significance the incidence carries no threat or violent connotation.

I do not wish to minimize the domestic upheaval now taking place in America, nor the violence that necessarily follows in its train. It simply does not seem particularly surprising that blacks are finally returning violence in kind, or that formerly nonviolent protesters are tired of being passively beaten up, or that working class whites violently resist the loss of the only barrier that keeps them from slipping to the bottom of the social hierarchy, or that fraternity boys beat up fellow students who seem unconventional to them. In fact all domestic violence pales before the violence we have created outside of our own borders, and it is on this violence that I would like to concentrate in this chapter. Indeed, it seems not unreasonable to suggest that it plays some role in all other forms, for is it not true that the leaders of a nation set the tone and style for lesser men? And if the leaders cannot abstain from the perpetration of violence and brutality who will be able to?

Curiously enough, our willingness to acknowledge the ubiquity of domestic violence has never extended itself to the international sphere. Included in our country-bumpkin self-image was the notion that we always became embroiled in foreign conflicts against our will, seduced from our pacific pursuits. Expansionist drives against Mexico and Spain were glossed over, along with our uniquely bloody civil war, our brutal suppression of Philippine independence, and our strong-arm tactics in Latin America. The Bay of Pigs, the Dominican episode, and the Vietnam war—despite a whole new vocabulary of self-deception ("escalation," "pacification")—have unraveled this illusion.

What most disturbs thoughtful Americans about Vietnam is the prevalence of genocidal thought patterns in our approach to the conflict. By this I do not mean merely remarks by wild-eyed generals about "dropping a nuke," or frustrated soldiers talking about "paving the country over from one end to the other." Official policy may be expressed in more restrained language but the euphemisms do not entirely hide the same genocidal assumptions. "Rooting out the infrastructure," for example, means essentially that you no longer kill only soldiers carrying weapons, but every civilian who might be related to or sympathetic to those soldiers. Since in a civil war there is no way of telling this at a glance, it comes to mean killing everyone in a specified area.

In past wars, casualties have been viewed as ancillary to some other goal for which the war was being fought. Even the Nazis were primarily interested in acquiring territory and making converts. For us the body count has become an end in itself: each day we tally how many killings we have achieved (ignoring, in the process, how many enemies we have engendered among the neutral living). The implicit assumption of the enemy-fatality statistics is "so many today, so many tomorrow, and one day we will have killed all the Communists in the world and will live happily ever after." This transfer of killing from a means to an end in itself constitutes a practical definition of genocide. Defoliation, napalm, and cluster bombs are designed to exterminate a population, not to win ground, liberate, convert, or pacify.

Media reports reflect this pattern of thought. A soldier boasted in the press of killing over two hundred people. Another, discovered to be underaged, protested (this was the newspaper headline): "I Can Kill As Well As Anybody." And when the bombing of North Vietnam was resumed after a lull in January, 1966, a Boston paper carried the cheery headline, "Bombs Away"!

Americans have always been a people with marked genocidal proclivities: our systematic extermination of the Indian, the casual killing of American blacks during and after slavery, and our indifference to dropping an atomic bomb on a large civilian populace —we are, after all, the *only* people ever to have used such a weapon —reflect this attitude. We have long had a disturbing tendency to see nonwhites—particularly Orientals—as nonhuman, and to act accordingly. In recent years this courtesy has been extended to the peoples of Communist nations generally, so that at present the majority of the earth's population are candidates for extermination on one count or the other. But white Communist countries usually enjoy the benefit of our fantasy that the people in those countries are ordinary humans enslaved by evil despots and awaiting liberation. When some event—such as the Bay of Pigs fiasco—disconfirms this fantasy, we are simply bewildered and turn our attention elsewhere. The same disconfirmation in a country like Vietnam tends to activate the genocidal assumptions that never lie far beneath the surface of our attitude toward nonwhite nations.

But if this is true—if Americans have always been genocidal, then the Vietnam conflict does not require any special explanation. Every society that has achieved a position of preeminence in the world has shown a remarkable capacity for brutality and violence— you don't get to be the bully of the block without using your fists. I am arguing that Vietnam is different only because it occurred in the face of a host of what might be expected to be inhibiting factors —practical as well as moral—that have arisen in the past few decades. We know from vast experience, for example, that military force is ineffectual in changing attitudes, that air power is cruel but ineffectual against civilian populations, that colonial expeditionary forces are ineffectual against organized indigenous popular movements of any size, and that military dictators will not and cannot broaden their own base of support. We watched carefully while France failed, and then repeated all her mistakes on a larger scale.* We helped to establish international principles in the U.N., at Geneva, and at Nuremberg, which we then violated or ignored. We live in a society in which the cruelties of war can be exposed in every living room through mass media. We discuss and debate constantly the appearance of any instance anywhere in the world of inhumane treatment of one person by another. We stress that every human life is a thing of value. We live, in short, in a modern, secure, civilized world, in which a single isolated act of violence is a calamity, an outrage. Yet we engage in the mass slaughter of innocent persons by the most barbarous means possible and show no qualms about it (resistance to the war has been largely in terms of expense and, secondarily, the loss of *American* lives). Since we are no longer crude frontiersmen or hillbillies what leads us to condone such savagery? When one observes that we devote the lion's share of our national budget to war and destruction, that capable scientists are tied up in biological and chemical warfare research that would make Frankenstein and his science-fiction colleagues look like Doctor Doolittle, we cannot avoid asking the question, do Americans hate life? Has there ever been a people who have destroyed so many living things?

The precipitating stimulus for these questions is Frank Harvey's

---

* For some reason the escalation of failure has always been particularly popular with military lobbyists. When the war in the South failed they demanded to be allowed to bomb the North. When the bombing proved ineffectual they demanded that it be expanded. When poison gas proved ineffectual they demanded an increase in the amount and toxicity of gas used. The Pentagon here plays the part of the ne'er-do-well nephew who "borrows" our money, loses it at the racetrack, and when caught and confronted with his delinquency tries to brazen it out, saying: "Never mind how and why I got here, I've lost $500 of your money and you have to give me another $1000 so I can win it back."

The escalation of failure has respectable but inauspicious precedents: Athens, unable to defeat Sparta, invaded Syracuse, and extinguished herself as a dominant political power.

Air War—Vietnam, supplemented by Robert Crichton's thoughtful review.[1] As Crichton points out, Harvey's book is particularly compelling because he was a military writer chosen by the Pentagon to publicize the air war, and was given access to information and experiences an unsympathetic reporter could never obtain. But although the Pentagon's efforts to censor Harvey's remarks were ultimately unsuccessful, the book has received surprisingly little attention.

Before describing the varieties of extermination practiced in Vietnam we should perhaps dispose at the outset of one objection that might be raised. For some people, the fact that an individual or group has been defined as an enemy and a combatant justifies whatever horror one wishes to inflict upon him, and nothing in what follows will be viewed by these readers as worthy of note. Unfortunately, however, in Vietnam it is difficult or impossible to determine who the enemy is. We have been repeatedly trapped in our own rhetoric on this matter—initially by portraying ourselves as aiding a friendly Vietnamese majority against a small, alien, and sinister minority. This created the expectation that villages "liberated" from the Viet Cong would welcome us with open arms, as Paris did in World War II. When it turned out that they were not pleased to be rescued from their husbands, brothers, sons, and fathers, we burned their villages and destroyed their crops, and began to give increased emphasis to the idea of outside agencies, particularly the North Vietnamese. To a considerable extent our attack on North Vietnam can be traced to our unwillingness to admit that we are fighting the people in South Vietnam.

Fortunately, the Air Force does not deceive itself when it comes to the welfare of its downed pilots, who are advised that when hit they should try to crash into the sea, since "everybody on the ground in South or North Vietnam (when you [float] down in a parachute, at least) must be considered an enemy." Pilots are also briefed never to say anything against Ho Chi Minh in South Vietnam since he is their national hero. Yet knowing this, knowing that "killing Viet Cong" may mean shooting up a Saigon suburb; knowing that Arvin troops regularly smuggle or abandon ammunition to the Viet Cong; knowing that north of Saigon there are almost no Arvin troops, and that those that do exist may at any time be

suddenly recalled to quell a popular uprising, American troops seldom combine these data to draw the obvious conclusion—although
they admire the Viet Cong, wonder why they keep fighting against
such overwhelming technological superiority (especially when
many are as young as 12 years old), and wish they were allies: "If
we had them on our side, we'd wrap up this war in about a
month."[2]

The examples that follow, then, do not concern merely an armed
enemy force but an entire populace, whose relation to this force
is highly ambiguous. Should a Vietnamese farmer shoot back when
bombed and strafed, he is retroactively defined as "Viet Cong." He
is certainly, by now, anti-American.

Pilots learn their trade in the Delta, where there are no trees for
the peasants to hide under, and no anti-aircraft fire. It is so safe for
Americans that one pilot described it as "a rabbit shoot." The
young pilot "learns how it feels to drop bombs on human beings
and watch huts go up in a boil of orange flame when his aluminum
napalm tanks tumble into them. He gets hardened to pressing the
firing button and cutting people down like little cloth dummies, as
they sprint frantically under him." If he is shot down, there are
so many planes in the area that his average time on the ground (or
in the sea) is only eleven minutes. Thus it is a very one-sided war
here—as Harvey says, the Vietnamese have about as much chance
against American air power as we would have against spaceships
with death rays.[3] This training prepares American pilots for the
genocidal pattern of the overall war. It does not prepare them,
however, for the slightly more equal contest of bombing North
Vietnam in the face of anti-aircraft fire, where planes are lost in
huge numbers and downed pilots are captured by the enemy.
American pilots were most anxious to bomb North Vietnam until
they had actually experienced the ground fire, at which point their
motivation lessened markedly. It became difficult, in fact, to man
these missions. According to Harvey, the Tactical Air Command in
Vietnam loses a squadron of pilots a month for noncombat reasons.
Killing in a dubious war is apparently much more palatable than
getting killed, and Americans are not used to fighting with anything
approaching equal odds (imagine our outrage if the North Vietnamese bombed us back). In the Delta, pilots seem surprised and al-

most indignant when their massive weaponry is countered with small-arms fire. One pilot, asked if he had killed anyone on a mission, replied: "Yeah–thirty, maybe forty. . . . Those little mothers were shooting back today, though." We are reminded of the old French chestnut:

Cet animal est très méchant,
Quand on l'attaque, il se défend.

As Crichton points out, Americans have become so accustomed to what Harvey estimates as 1000 to 1 firepower odds that they come to feel it is their inherent right to kill people without retaliation.[4]

The administration of extermination in the Delta is highly decentralized. Decisions are made by forward air controllers (FACs) who fly about looking for signs of "guerilla activity" (which in most cases can be translated as "life"). "They cruise around over the Delta like a vigilante posse, holding the power of life and death over the Vietnamese villagers living beneath." The weapons that they can call in have an unfortunate tendency to kill indiscriminately. There is napalm, which rolls and splatters about over a wide area burning everything burnable that it touches, suffocating those who try to escape by hiding in tunnels, pouring in and incinerating those who hide in family bomb shelters under their huts. Napalm is a favorite weapon, according to Harvey, and is routinely used on rows of houses, individual farms, and rice paddies. "Daisy cutters," or bombs which explode in the water, are also used against peasants hiding in rice paddies. White phosphorous bombs are another incendiary used, and Harvey saw a man in a civilian hospital with a piece of phosphorus in his flesh, still burning. Harvey considers the deadliest weapon to be cluster bomb units (CBUs), which contain tiny bomblets expelled over a wide area. With this device a pilot could "lawnmower for considerable distances, killing or maiming anybody on a path several hundred feet wide and many yards long." The CBUs are particularly indiscriminate since many have delayed action fuses, and go off when the "suspect," whose appearance provoked the FAC observer to trigger off this holocaust, is far away, and the victims being "lawnmowered" are children playing about in a presumably safe area or peasants going about their daily work. Victims who survive must sometimes undergo rather unusual surgery—if hit in the abdomen it must be slit from top to bottom and the intestines spilled out onto a table and fingered for fragments. With one type of CBU a plane can shred an area a mile long and a quarter of a mile wide with more than a million steel fragments. It is difficult to reconcile this kind of indiscriminate killing with speeches about "winning the hearts and minds of the Vietnamese people."[5]

The degree of initiative granted the FACs amounts to a mandate for genocide. If a FAC sees nothing suspicious below he is entitled to employ "Recon by smoke" or "Recon by fire." In the first case he drops a smoke grenade and if anyone runs from the explosion they are presumed guilty, and napalmed (if they run into their house) or machine-gunned (if they take to the rice paddies). "Recon by fire" is based on the same principle except that CBUs are used instead of smoke grenades, so that if the victims do *not* run they will be killed anyway. These techniques are a bit reminiscent of the ducking stool used in earlier centuries to test potential witches: if the woman was not a witch she drowned—if she did not drown this proved she was a witch and she was burned to death. As Harvey points out, American front-line volunteers enjoy shooting and killing, and do it more effectively than most people. It is the deadly efficiency of the slaughter that impresses us, and the at times bewildering overkill—dropping bombs on individuals or using multi-million-dollar planes to "barbecue" peasant huts. When a lone farmer standing in a field manages to hit one of these over-armed pilots with a rifle shot it is impossible to stifle a cheer. But the more usual result is for the upstart to be shredded by machine-gun bullets (fired at the rate of 100 rounds per *second*) and literally to disintegrate to a pile of bloody rags. This enthusiasm for killing was exhibited in an impersonal way by a pilot who suggested starting at the DMZ and killing every man, woman, and child in North Vietnam; and more personally by a "Huey" pilot who described killing a single man: "I ran that little mother all over the place hosing him with guns but somehow or other we just didn't hit him. Finally he turned on us and stood there facing us with his rifle. We really busted his ass then. Blew him up like a toy balloon" (the Huey gunship is a three-man helicopter equipped with six machine guns, rockets, and grenade-launchers).[6]

Harvey met a few FACs, at least, who did not enjoy killing civilians. One advertised his guilt feelings and was relieved of duty. Another, who apparently had learned the lesson of Nuremberg, questioned an order to shell a peaceful village filled with women and children. When the order was reaffirmed he directed the artillery fire into an empty rice paddy. For some pilots, however, their remoteness from their targets protects them from such awareness. B52 bombers, flying from Guam, over 2500 miles away, or from Thailand, dropping bombs from 40,000 feet so that they cannot be seen or heard from below, can wipe out an entire valley. In one of these "saturation" or "carpet" raids, fifty square miles of jungle can suddenly explode into flame without warning, from a rain of fire bombs. These raids are frequent, and in the areas they strike, nothing will live, animal or human, friend or enemy. It is almost as effective on plants and animals as defoliation, which kills three hundred acres in four minutes (the motto of the "Ranch Hands" is "Only You Can Prevent Forests"), probably not much more expensive (it costs almost two million dollars to keep a single plane defoliating for twenty-four hours), and a great deal more inclusive.[7]

Whenever American atrocities are discussed the answer is often given that the Viet Cong also commit atrocities, which is a little like saying that when an elephant steps on a mouse the mouse is equally aggressive when it bites the elephant's foot. A terrorist bomb is not equivalent to a B52 raid, nor the sadistic murder of a captured FAC (naturally the most hated of fliers) the equivalent of a CBU drop. With our overwhelming arsenal of grotesque weapons should go some minimal trace of responsibility. The Viet Cong are fighting for their existence while our pilots in the Delta are amusing themselves with impunity—their merry euphemisms, such as "hosing" and "barbecuing" express this freedom.

Implicit in the atrocity equation, of course, is the assumption that American lives are precious and other peoples' lives are of no more account than ants. The fantastic disproportion in firepower (". . . it is a little exaggerated . . . We're applying an $18,000,000 solution to a $2 problem. But, still, one of the little mothers *was* firing at us") is justified in terms of saving American lives. At times Harvey seems to be describing some kind of aristocratic adventure: when Major Kasler was shot down over North Vietnam so many American planes were sent out to rescue him that they had difficulty avoiding collisions. But not all of the excess can be attributed to this concern: when a Huey gunship empties its ammunition into total darkness ("nobody will ever know if we hit anything but we certainly did a lot of shooting"), or a B52 rains bombs all over a forest in the hope that perhaps some Viet Cong are hiding in it, this can hardly be defined as saving American lives. It is simply gratuitous aggression, taking a form that owes much to the Toilet Assumption. Furthermore, the excessive American firepower and its more grisly manifestations often backfire, and destroy those same expensive lives they are supposed to protect. Captured CBUs are made into booby traps and blow off American limbs. A large supply of our "Bouncing Betty" mines (so called because they are made to leap up and explode in the face), abandoned to the Viet Cong by the Arvins, have caused what Harvey calls "sickening" casualties to our own troops. Our planes collide because there are so many. Dragon ships are melted by their own flares. Fliers are endangered when the Navy and the Air Force try to "out-sortie" each other. Fliers sometimes napalm our own troops. After the *Forrestal* disaster a flier expressed momentary repugnance at having to drop bombs and napalm on North Vietnam after seeing what they had done to our own men.[8]

When all is said and done, American lives, while accorded an extraordinary value relative to those of Vietnamese civilians, still take a back seat relative to the death-dealing machinery they serve. Aircraft carriers, for example, are careless of human life even under the best of conditions, remote from the field of battle. Planes disappear under the sea with their pilots rather easily (the cost of planes lost through landing and takeoff accidents would have financed the poverty program), men are ignited by jet fuel, or devoured by jet engines, or run over by flight deck equipment, or blown into the sea by jet winds, or cut in half by arresting cables, or decapitated by helicopter blades. Even safety devices seem to be geared less to human needs than to the demands of the machinery: pilots ejected from F-4s regularly receive broken backs or other severe spinal injuries.[9] The arguments about Viet Cong atrocities and saving American lives become ludicrous in the face of the daily reality of America's life-destroying technology.

What enables civilized humans to become brutalized in this way? Why are not more of them sickened and disillusioned as men so often have been in the past when forced to engage in one-sided slaughter?

There are really two different types of human extermination involved in Vietnam, and they perhaps require two different kinds of explanation. First, there is extermination such as the Huey troops engage in—extermination at close range, in which the killer can see (and enjoy, apparently) the blood he sheds. Second, and far more common, there is extermination at a distance, in which the extent of the killing is so vast that the killer tends to think in terms of areas on a map rather than individuals. In neither case is the victim perceived as a person (such a perception would make modern war impossible), but in the first case the killer at least sees the immediate consequences of his act, whereas in the second case he does not. The "close-range" killers in Vietnam are confronting *something*, even if it has little to do with the root dissatisfactions in their lives (one of the Huey pilots in Harvey's book reenlisted because he could not tolerate the demands of civilian life).

But for the "long-range" killers—which in a sense includes all of us—do we need any explanation at all? Governments have always tried to keep their soldiers from thinking of "the enemy" as human, by portraying them as monsters and by preventing contact ("fraternization") with them, and modern weaponry makes it very easy for anyone to be a mass killer without much guilt or stress. Flying in a plane far above an impersonally defined target and pressing some buttons to turn fifty square miles into a sea of flame is less traumatic to the average middle-class American boy than inflicting a superficial bayonet wound on a single male soldier.* The flier

* A wilderness-survival expert once pointed out to me that army training in hand-to-hand combat virtually ignores the body's own weaponry: ripping out the windpipe or jugular of one's opponent with one's teeth, for example,

cannot see the women and children being horribly burned to death —they have no meaning to him. Violence-at-a-distance, then, occurs simply because it is so easy—just another expression of the Toilet Assumption.

This is a necessary but not a sufficient condition for violence at a distance. Everyone who has a gun does not use it, and everyone who has an atom bomb does not drop it. Furthermore, one must explain why America has developed more elaborate, complex, and grotesque techniques for exterminating people at a distance than any nation in the history of the world. Our preference for slaughter from the air certainly has some practical basis in the need to insulate carefully reared soldiers from the horrors they cause, but practical considerations alone hardly account for the fiendishness of our weaponry. Can this all result from the miseries and frustrations of American life? Or the logical unfolding of institutional processes? Why does a peasant defending his home, his family, and his property arouse such massive retaliatory responses from American forces, and why are they equipped for genocide?

Other nations have weapons (perhaps less wildly elaborated than ours) capable of causing mass destruction at a distance, but they have not been utilized to any extent. There must therefore be some special factor to account for this uniquely American characteristic. Perhaps it is not an accident that Americans engage so intensively in killing from a distance—perhaps the distance itself carries special meaning. Perhaps Americans enjoy the mass impersonal killing of people who cannot fight back because they themselves suffer mass impersonal injuries from mechanical forces against which they, too, are powerless.

There are, indeed, two ways in which this occurs. The first arises from our tendency to handle interpersonal conflict by increasing individual autonomy, which, as we have seen, simply attenuates the directness of these conflicts. The clashes between people that are thereby avoided rebound upon us by a very circuitous route. We create elaborate mechanisms to avoid conflict with our neighbor

---

might be in many situations the most simple and expedient way of disabling him, but well-brought-up Americans shun such intimate contact with the victims of their mutilations.

and find as a result that we are beleaguered by some impersonal far-off agency. When we fight with our neighbor we can yell at each other and feel some relief, perhaps even make it up or find a solution. But there is little satisfaction in yelling at a traffic jam, or a faulty telephone connection, or an erroneous IBM card, or any of the thousand petty (and some not so petty) irritations to which Americans are daily subject. Most of these irritations are generated by vast impersonal institutions to which the specific individuals we encounter are only vaguely connected ("I only work here"). We not only feel helpless in relation to their size and complexity, but the difficulty of locating the source of responsibility for the problem is so overwhelming that attempts at redress are often abandoned even by middle-class persons, while the poor seldom even try. This is a situation that modern comedians have become adroit at satirizing, but aside from laughter and vague expressions of futile exasperation at "the system" we can do little to relieve our feelings. The energy required to avoid even the most obvious forms of exploitation by commercial enterprises in our society would not permit the individual to lead a normal active life. Like Looking-Glass Country, it takes all the running one can do to stay in the same place.

Powerlessness has always been the common lot of most of mankind, but in a preindustrial age one could at least locate the source of injury. If a nobleman beat you, robbed you, or raped your womenfolk you hated the nobleman. If a hospital removes a kidney instead of an appendix, or when there is only one kidney to remove (accidents that occur far more often than most people imagine, particularly to ward patients), whom do we hate? The orderly who brought the wrong record? The doctor who failed to notice discrepancies? The poor filing system?

The more we attempt to solve problems through increased autonomy the more we find ourselves at the mercy of these mysterious, impersonal, and remote mechanisms that we have ourselves created. Their indifference is a reflection of our own. Our preference for violence at a distance is thus both an expression of and a revenge against this process. We send bombers to destroy "Communism" in Vietnam instead of meeting our needs for collaboration and coordination at home. But part of the motivation for that particular kind of savagery comes from the very remoteness involved. Remote and unknown enemies have a special meaning to us—we associate them with the unknown forces that beset us. In other words, the very fact of Vietnam's remoteness and strangeness increases our hatred —our willingness to use sadistic and genocidal instruments. This becomes clear when we think of Vietnam in relation to Cuba: both are small countries involving no real threat to our power, but one is near and one is far, and we would hesitate using in Cuba the instruments of mass destruction that we employ in Vietnam.

The second process is closely tied to this one, and has to do with the way we arrange our opposing needs for stability and change. All societies, optimally, must allow for both change and stability, since: (a) effective adaptation to the environment requires both modification and consolidation of existing responses; (b) social integration depends both upon the preservation and upon the periodic dissolution of existing structural differentiation; and (c) personal happiness rests upon both familiarity and novelty in everyday life. Every society evolves patterns for attempting to realize these mutually incompatible needs.

Our society, as many have pointed out, has traditionally handled the problem by giving completely free rein to technological change and opposing the most formidable obstacles to social change. Since, however, technological change in fact forces social changes upon us, this has had the effect of abdicating all control over our social environment to a kind of whimsical deity. While we think of ourselves as a people of change and progress, masters of our environment and our fate, we are no more entitled to this designation than the most superstitious savage, for our relation to change is entirely passive. We poke our noses out the door each day and wonder breathlessly what new disruptions technology has in store for us. We talk of technology as the servant of man, but it is a servant that now dominates the household, too powerful to fire, upon whom everyone is helplessly dependent. We tiptoe about and speculate upon his mood. What will be the effects of such-and-such an invention? How will it change our daily lives? We never ask, do we *want* this, is it worth it? (We did not ask ourselves, for example, if the trivial conveniences offered by the automobile could really offset the calamitous disruption and depersonalization of our lives that it brought about.) We simply say "You can't stop progress" and shuffle back inside.

We pride ourselves on being a "democracy" but we are in fact slaves. We submit to an absolute ruler whose edicts and whims we never question. We watch him carefully, hang on his every word; for technology is a harsh and capricious king, demanding prompt and absolute obedience. We laugh at the Luddites (Nat Turners in the struggle for human parity with the machine) but they were the last human beings seriously to confront this issue. Since then we have passively surrendered to every degradation, every atrocity, every enslavement that our technological ingenuity has brought about. We laugh at the old lady who holds off the highway bull-dozers with a shotgun, but we laugh because we are Uncle Toms. We try to outdo each other in singing the praises of the oppressor, although in fact the value of technology in terms of human satisfaction remains at best undemonstrated. For when evaluating its effects we always adopt the basic assumptions and perspective of technology itself, and never examine it in terms of the totality of human experience. We say this or that invention is valuable because it generates other inventions—because it is a means to some other means—not because it achieves an ultimate human end. We play down the "side effects" that so often become the main effects and completely negate any alleged benefits. The advantages of *all* technological "progress" will after all be totally outweighed the moment nuclear war breaks out (an event which, given the inadequacy of precautions and the number of fanatical fingers close to the trigger, is only a matter of time unless radical changes are made).

Let me make clear what I am *not* saying here. I do not believe in the noble savage and I am not advocating any brand of bucolic romanticism. I do not want to put an end to machines, I only want to remove them from their position of mastery, to restore human beings to a position of equality and initiative. As a human I must protest that being able to sing and eat watermelon all day is no compensation for being beaten, degraded, and slaughtered at random, and this is the nature of our current relationship to our technological order.

Nor am I attributing all these ills to capitalism. The Soviet Union and other planned economies are as enslaved as we. They may be allowed more freedom in working out the details of the commands given them, but they seem to have no more say in the basic policy-making. Technology makes core policy in every industrialized nation, and the humans adjust as best they can.

The much-vaunted "freedom" of American life is thus an illusion, one which underlies the sense of spuriousness so many Americans feel about their basic institutions. We are free to do only what we are told, and we are "told" not by a human master but by a mechanical construction.

But how can we be the slaves of technology—is not technology merely an extension of, a creation of, ourselves? This is only metaphorically true. The forces to which we submit so abjectly were not generated by ourselves but by our ancestors—what we create will in turn rule our progeny. It takes a certain amount of time for the social effects of technological change to make their appearance, by which time a generation has usually passed.

Science-fiction writers have long been fascinated with the notion of being able to create material objects just by imagining them, and have built novels, stories, and films around this idea. Actually, it is merely an exaggeration of what normally takes place. Technology is materialized fantasy. We are ruled today by the material manifestations of the fantasies of previous generations.

It is for this reason that the concept of the tyrannical father has never disappeared from American culture. Whereas in everyday family life the despotic patriarch is (and probably always has been, although each generation of Americans imagines the past to have been different)[10] a rare curiosity, it is an *idea* with which every American is on terms of intimate familiarity. If the personal authorities with whom Americans come into earliest and most intense contact are warm and benign, what is the basis of the other concept?

This question was raised two decades ago by Wolfenstein and Leites in their brilliant analysis of the cultural preoccupations revealed by American films.[11] They observed that in the typical popular film the hero's father was portrayed as a kindly, bumbling, ineffectual figure, but that the hero usually came into conflict with another male authority—a cattle baron, captain of industry, political leader, or racketeer—who was powerful, evil, despotic, iron-willed, and aggressive, quite unlike the kindly old father (who played the same inconsequential role he plays in TV situation comedies). Wolfenstein and Leites saw this discrepancy as revealing deeper and more primitive Oedipal fantasies, from the perspective of a child so small that any authority seems overpowering.

I would suggest, however, that this image derives some of its continuing force and appeal from the realities of everyday adult experience. We treat technology as if it were a fierce patriarch—we are deferential, submissive, and alert to its demands. We feel spasms of hatred toward it, and continually make fun of it, but do little to challenge its rule. Technology has inherited the fantasy of the authoritarian father. Furthermore, since the technological environment that rules, frustrates, and manipulates us is a materialization of the wishes of our forefathers, it is quite reasonable to say that technology *is* the authoritarian father in our society. The American father can be a good-natured slob in the home precisely because he is so ruthless toward the nonhuman environment, leveling, uprooting, filling in, building up, tearing down, blowing up, tunneling under. This ruthlessness affects his children only indirectly, as the deranged environment afflicts the eyes, ears, nose, and nervous system of the next generation. But it affects them nonetheless. Through this impersonal intermediary we inflict our will upon our children, and punish them for our generous indulgence—our child-oriented, self-sacrificing behavior. It is small wonder that the myth of the punitive patriarch stays alive.

From this viewpoint, then, delegating to technology the role of punitive patriarch is another example of the first process we described: the tendency to avoid interpersonal conflict by compartmentalization and a false illusion of autonomy—to place impersonal mechanisms between and around people and imagine that we have created a self-governing paradise. It is a kind of savage joke in its parental form. We say: "Look, I am an easy-going, good-natured, affectionate father. I behave in a democratic manner and treat you like a person, never pulling rank. As to all those roads and wires and machines and bombs and complex bureaucratic institutions out there, don't concern yourself about them—this is my department."

But when the child grows up he discovers the fraud. He learns that he is a slave to his father's unconscious and unplanned whims—that the area of withheld power was crucial. He becomes angry and rebels, saying, "You were not what you pretended, and I cannot be what you encouraged me to be." He attacks "the system" and authority everywhere, trying to find the source of the deception, and using techniques that reflect his commitment to what his father deceived him into thinking he was—a person. But by this time he has also learned the system of avoiding conflict through impersonal mechanism and is ready to inflict the same deception on his own children.

Margaret Mead describes a mild, peaceful tribe—the Arapesh—that shares this device with us.[12] Whenever an Arapesh is angry at one of his compatriots he never attacks him directly. Instead he gets some of his "dirt" (body excretions, food leavings, etc.) and gives it to a sorcerer from the plains tribe nearby, who may or may not use it to destroy the victim through magic. If the man dies years later his death will be attributed to this sorcery, though the quarrel be long since forgotten. The Arapesh see themselves as incapable of killing each other—they do not even know any black magic. Death comes from the plains.

Our enlightened civilization proceeds on precisely the same model. We love and indulge our children, and would never dream of hurting them. If they are poisoned, bombed, gassed, burned, or whatever, it is surely not our fault, since we do not even know how to manipulate these objects. The danger comes from outside. Perhaps long ago we did something to deliver them into these impersonal hands, but we have forgotten, and in any case it is not our responsibility. Technology, in other words, is our plains sorcerer.

The joy in killing a far-off enemy, then, derives additional strength from this configuration. The "enemy" is distant and impersonal. Since injury comes to us from remote sources we must find a remote victim on which to wreak our vengeance.

Since the "real" enemy is our technologically strangled environment (ultimately of course ourselves and our ancestors) it may seem ironic that we avenge ourselves by killing an impoverished people who had not experienced this environment before we inflicted it upon them. We have utilized what oppresses us to oppress other human beings. But this has always been true of downtrodden classes —afraid to attack the oppressor they take out their rage on each other. Blacks have for centuries squandered their rebellion in fraternal slaughter, and other examples can be found in every period in history. Human beings as a whole, enslaved by their Frankenstein-monsters, behave no differently. And it is even less likely that the people of the United States and Vietnam will ever join together and consign the napalm, defoliants, Hueys, CBUs, and all other life-hating implements to oblivion. Misery loves company more than its own end. And Americans love machines more than life itself.

*   *   *

When young blacks began to turn their aggression against their oppressors no one displayed more fierce disapproval than some of their own elders. As the fathers brought their sons to take their place in line for the beatings, degradation, and humiliation that were to be their lot in life the sons stepped out of the queue and declined to participate. The elders became angry and shouted that this was the way the world was and they must learn to accept it— how else could they get a job shining shoes or cleaning toilets?

A comparable rage is displayed today by older victims of technological oppression against youth who challenge this oppression, and a similar argument takes place: How can you expect to emulate my miserable life if you don't accept oppression? And the answer comes back, muted by the affection, gratitude, and guilt the parents' love and self-sacrifice have earned: "I don't want to be like you."

The most dramatic expression of this rage is the "police riot," a term invented after the 1968 Democratic Convention to describe the habit policemen have of smashing, with rather too much enthusiasm, the heads of young people. But, as many people have pointed out, the police function, however inelegantly, as agents of community attitudes, and if they did not feel that the community supported their actions they probably would not occur.* If blacks

---

* Many of the assassinations of recent years—the two Kennedys, Martin Luther King, Malcolm X—may be understood in the same way: as actions triggered by a sense of latent community approval. Probably there is always a sizable pool of potential assassins—men disturbed and desperate enough

50   THE PURSUIT OF LONELINESS

are shot at or arrested or beaten merely for walking in a suburban white neighborhood, it is because most residents in that neighborhood tend to see a burglar or rapist in every black face. And if our college-age children are beaten and maced this act also reflects accurately our vicious resentment of their youth and their rejection of our values and life-style. In my own community the same week brought a series of raids on students smoking marijuana in the privacy of their apartments and a refusal by the police chief to guarantee coverage of a dangerous grade school crossing (at which a six-year-old child had recently been killed) on the grounds that the Force had more important things to do. That a small child's life is considered of less importance than preventing college students from enjoying themselves may seem bizarre, but may also be an accurate reflection of community priorities.

It might be objected that police riots go far beyond majority community attitudes in intensity. But how, then, can we account for the thumping popular approval accorded Mayor Daley and the Chicago police after the convention riots, when some of the police violence was shown on television? Or the efforts of a small Midwestern town to send an English youth to jail for six months for wearing his hair in the English style? Or the efforts of a wealthy suburban community to send dedicated young high school teachers

---

both to kill a public figure and to run a very high risk of capture. When a rash of assassinations occurs we must assume that the threshold between fantasy and action has been lowered somehow—that some restraining pressure has been removed.

It is probably not accidental that these recent victims were all rather young men—not conservative father figures trying to retain power and preserve old ways, but young liberals or radicals trying to effect social change. If we make the rather safe assumption that the potential assassin is conflicted about authority, the assassination of such men satisfies both their rebellious and submissive tendencies: the assassin does not really kill authority, he kills in the *name* of authority. To one in his state of mind the hate exuded by his elders is a kind of permission. Not that the act is suggested to the assassin—it is rather that the constraining atmosphere that might have prevented his seriously entertaining the idea in the case of a conservative leader is lacking in the case of one who himself represents a challenge to established ways. In the anger and hate of older people around him the assassin finds a fertile soil in which the idea can grow instead of being extinguished.

to prison for presenting a contemporary black drama that contained the word "fuck"? (The latter incident evoked a town meeting, during which the class valedictorian rose to defend the play; upon his own use of the offending word the audience screamed "Kill him!" and a policeman was called to drag him away, amid total pandemonium.) The past ten years have demonstrated so frequently how easy it is for a wealthy and respectable WASP community to descend to the level of a lynch mob that we can no longer attribute any special qualities of brutality to working-class policemen. The general view of both groups is that violence must be met with violence, and violence of the first sort is defined as "anything that makes me angry or stirs me up in any way."

But what is it that stirs people up so? Why does the older generation hate its children with such vehemence? I would like to postpone this specific question to the next chapter, in which intergenerational relationships will be considered in more detail. And some aspects of the general American proneness to respond savagely to exciting stimuli can only be understood with reference to issues that will be discussed in Chapter Four. A partial answer can be found, however, in our discussion of needs for stability and change. Because Americans have submitted so passively to the havoc wreaked by technological change, they have had to convince themselves that their obsequiousness is right and good and appropriate. Any challenge to the technological-over-social priority threatens to expose the fact that Americans have lost their manhood and their capacity to control their environment. So long as the priority is unchallenged and unmentioned, the human surrender involved need not be confronted. But youth is increasingly saying: "What about the people? Why have you abdicated your birthright to hardware?" It is a humiliating question, and humiliating questions tend to be answered with blows.

Furthermore, the social changes wrought by technological change are so vast and shattering and we are kept so off-balance by them that the desire for independent social change (that is, change produced by human needs rather than technology) appears not as a solution and the assumption of control, but as still another disruptive force. It is like the inhabitants of an occupied country, who say to their militants, "don't fight the enemy, it will just bring more massive retaliation down upon us." The predominant feeling is that there is more change than anybody can tolerate already, so how can anyone even *consider* a radical reevaluation of the whole system. Or, to paraphrase a cartoon by Mell Lazarus: "I know I need to see a psychiatrist, but the idea scares me too much now—I'll go when I'm less anxious." Apparently, the idea not only scares us—it makes us mad enough to kill somebody.

3

Women and children first

Women may not be serious, but at least they're not a
damned fool!
SNOW WHITE[1]

Your mother's ghost stands at your shoulder,
Face like ice—a little bit colder—
CROSBY

Black, white, green, red,
Can I take my friend to bed?
LENNON AND MC CARTNEY

A curious event of the late sixties was the popularity of the film,
The Graduate, the viewing of which became almost a ritual for
a wide spectrum of middle-class youth, who went to see it over and
over. It was a brilliant film, constructed almost entirely of movie
clichés, but many middle-aged reviewers were disturbed by its
fusion of satire and naïve romanticism. With the intolerance for
ambiguity that characterizes both the generation and the genre,
some critics attempted either to maintain that it was really *all* satire,
or to dismiss it as basically callow.

The satire is largely associated with the more modern aspects of
the film; reflecting intergenerational hostility, its sources and consequences. But the heart of the film is its celebration of the old American dream of love triumphant over culture. One might even say
that it is a revival and a reformation of that Dream. Like Christianity, the Dream has always borne an almost antithetical relation
to the everyday life of the society in which it is embedded, yet has

53

still managed to dominate attitudes and even behavior within certain limited spheres. And like Christianity, the Dream became tarnished by this peculiar position in which it found itself.

Mike Nichols, the director of the film, was thus the Martin Luther of the Dream, reviving it and purifying it; clarifying, through satire, its ambiguous relation to the total culture, and restoring its original naïve form. It is of no consequence that the hero and his bride will become corrupted as time goes by. What is important is that the confrontation has taken place and Love has won, however briefly. *The Graduate*, like its paler predecessors, is a ritual of purification and cleansing, a celebration of the *capacity* of feeling to triumph over pattern. The interruption of a wedding ceremony—always a popular theme in American films—is not merely a suspense gimmick. It is what the film is all about: the battle between social forms and human feeling. And it is important that human feelings should occasionally win—as important as occasional epiphanies and miracles are for religion. In our society this issue is a matter of life and death (of the society, if not the individual).

In earlier films the basic conflict was usually attenuated, revolving almost exclusively around the question of choosing the more romantic and less conventional of two prospective marital partners. The stop-the-wedding element tended to be approached either comically or in a very muted way (i.e., no disruption of the ceremony). *The Graduate* moves up to its climax with cinematic clichés so densely packed that we feel we have seen the film before. Once in the church, however, we find that the years' accumulations of compromises and dilutions have been ruthlessly cut away. The hero makes no attempt whatever to cover or mask his feelings, the ceremony is totally and irretrievably shattered, and the hero must physically battle the representatives of society's forms. In this scene the old theme is presented with a baldness so complete that it becomes new and revolutionary.

When an old theme is revived in its true form, stripped of its routinizations and redefinitions, it always seems shocking. Raw and literal Christianity has this kind of impact. That *The Graduate* achieved popular success therefore implies some change in values (middle-aged people tended to object to the church scene, while most young people did not). The major change seems to me to be a strengthening of the feeling side of the human-need-versus-social-form conflict. For the older generation rituals, ceremonies, and social institutions have an intrinsic validity which makes them intimidating—a validity which takes priority over human events. One would hesitate to disrupt a serious social occasion for even the most acute and fateful need unless it could be justified in social rather than personal terms. Doris Lessing and Shelley Berman have both observed, in the case of people confronted with aircraft whose integrity has been cast in doubt, that most people would quietly die rather than "make a scene."

The younger generation experiences a greater degree of freedom from this allegiance. They do not see social occasions as automatically having intrinsic and sovereign validity. Their attitude is more secular—social formality is deferred to only when human concerns are not pressing. A well-brought-up young man like the hero of *The Graduate* would have tended, thirty years ago, to stand passively watching while his personal disaster took place—thus the church scene at that time would have seemed much less realistic (or else the hero defined as severely disturbed). Indeed, much of the older cinematic comedy made use of this meek deference—we recall the cops-and-robbers chases in which both participants would briefly interrupt their frantic efforts in order to stand at attention while the flag or a funeral procession passed by.

This change is responsible both for the character of radical protest in the sixties and for the angry responses of older people to it. Sitting-in at a segregated restaurant, occupying a campus building, lying down in front of vehicles, pouring blood in office files, and all of the imaginative devices emerging from modern protest movements depend heavily on a willingness to make a scene—not to be intimidated by a social milieu. And this is precisely what so enrages their elders, who are shocked not so much by the students' radicalism as by their bad form. That students should be rude to a public figure is more important to their elders than that the public figure is sending their children to their deaths in an evil cause. Students faced with situations in which existing practices are having disastrous consequences (killing people, destroying neighborhoods, cheating the poor, stultifying the minds of children, starving or brutalizing people, or whatever) are skeptical when told they should at all costs go through proper channels, knowing that such channels are typically ineffectual or prohibitively slow.* To be told it is better to kill or be killed than to be rude or make a public scene arouses much youthful bitterness and disillusionment, deftly captured in the protest song, "It Isn't Nice."

A part of this mistrust is unfounded. The young assume that their elders are attempting to deceive them with this talk of proper channels—that it is deliberate obstruction, since the elders know that "proper channels" are designed to negate rather than to facilitate change. But while this motive is undoubtedly present (much less consciously than the young assume), the reaction is based primarily on a horror of social uproar that the young simply do not experience and cannot comprehend. The elders' notion that radical leaders are "just trying to get their names in the papers" expresses their own bafflement at the contrast.

Yet the change is one that the elders themselves created, for it is based on child-oriented family patterns. Europeans have always felt that American parents paid far too much regard to their children's needs and far too little to the demands of adult social occasions; but Spock's emphasis on allowing the child to develop according to his own potential and needs (starting with the abandonment of the fixed schedule fad that enjoyed brief popularity in the twenties and thirties) focused the parents' attention on the child as a future adult, who could be more or less intelligent, creative, healthy, and personable according to how the parents behaved toward him. This was unlike the older view that the child had a fixed personality to which the parents tried to give a socially acceptable expression as best they could. The old method was based on the military drill model: you take people who are all basically different and get them to behave outwardly in a uniform manner, regardless of whether they are inwardly committed to this behavior or not. Thus there is a sharp distinction between the outer and inner spheres. The child or recruit is expected to harbor inner feelings

---

* At my own university recently a proposal for curriculum reform was passed after seven years of moving through "normal faculty procedures," and of course long after those students who had sought the change were graduated.

of rebellion or contempt, so long as these are not expressed outwardly.

The new method gives much more responsibility to the parents, for they must concern themselves with inner states. They are not merely trying to make the child well-behaved—for them personality is not a given, but something the parent can mold. The parents under the old method felt they had done their job well if the child was obedient, even if he turned out dull, unimaginative, surly, sadistic, and sexually incapacitated. Spockian parents feel that it is their responsibility to make their child into the most all-around perfect adult possible, which means paying a great deal of attention to his inner states and latent characteristics. The consequence of this is what is superficially defined as greater "permissiveness," but from an internal perspective is actually more totalitarian—the child no longer has a private sphere, but has his entire being involved with parental aspirations. What the child is *not* permitted to do is to take his own personality for granted.

Under the old system, for example, the parents would feel called upon to chastise a child defined as bright but lazy, and if they forced him to spend a fixed amount of time staring at a book— whether he learned anything or lost all interest in learning—they would feel justified and relieved of all moral responsibility for him ("I don't know why he's so bad, I beat him every day"). Today parents feel required not just to make him put in time but to make him motivated to learn.

The tradeoff for having his whole personality up for grabs is that the child's needs are paid much more attention. The old method demanded the subordination of these needs to social reality: for the most casual social encounter the parents would be willing to sacrifice the child's sense of truth and fair play ("kiss the nice lady"), bodily needs ("you'll just have to wait"), and even parental loyalty ("he's always stupid and shy with strangers"). For the parent who loved him to throw him to the dogs for something so trivial as etiquette makes a deep impression on the child. He sees the parent nurturant and protective in situations that seem much more important and dangerous, why not here? Since he cannot *see* anything so important as to justify this betrayal, all social situations tend to assume a sacred, awe-inspiring, inviolate quality. Since the

parents put this mysterious situation above all else, it comes to assume the same sovereignty for the child.

But Spock-oriented parents, absorbed with the goal of molding
the child's total character, were much less inclined to sacrifice the
child to the etiquette concerns of strangers. The artist working on
his masterpiece does not let guests use it to wipe their feet on. As a
result, their children have grown up to feel that human needs have
some validity of their own, and that social occasions are less sacred
than they appeared to earlier generations. As an SDS leader observed: ". . . educational institutions exist to fit [the student] to
the system and not *vice versa*, and that is a recognition that all of
his careful socialization to upper-middle-class values has ill-prepared
him to accept. We grew up feeling reasonably potent in influencing
our personal milieu; and without our parents' deeper needs for
economic and status security, we are in a much better position to
challenge a society that promises to make us impotent."[2] When
parents today enjoin their children to "face reality" (by which
they mean *social* reality) there is a double irony: first, because
their children have become so skillful at exposing how fictional
"reality" is, and second, because the parents themselves have never
been able to "face" this reality but have always been stared down
by it.

The hero of *The Graduate* is thus not intimidated by the wedding ceremony but wails out his pain, and the heroine, until then
bewitched by social forms, is disenchanted, rescued, and redeemed.
But what of the parents, who gave their children the power to confront what they are unable to resist themselves?* How do they react? In *The Graduate*, they show vindictive hatred, and this also is
a new departure, for in the older films the representatives of social
forms are merely left openmouthed, or slyly smiling (secretly
glad), or futilely shaking their fists. But here they attack viciously

---

* This unique power that parents have—to give their children attributes
they do not themselves possess—is perhaps the unconscious determinant of
an otherwise incomprehensible theme that appears so often in fairy tales:
that of the impoverished old parent or helper who gives the hero magic
gifts that could have made the giver himself wealthy and powerful but apparently did not.

and a true mêlée ensues. The hero fights off the mob by grabbing a large cross from the altar, beating them off with it, and then using it to bar the church door from the outside, permitting the couple to escape.

The cross incident is important for two reasons. First, the hero, by appropriating it, transforms it from a symbol of church convention and ritual to one of revolutionary Christianity, in which love takes precedence over ceremony. It is the final act of purification in the film, and it was shocking to adults who could not imagine religion being on the side of human feeling and against convention. But to young Christian activists it was not shocking at all, but a proper role for the cross to play. For was not Jesus himself impatient with traditional forms and rude to authority? Can it not be said of him that he acted in bad taste, and refused to seek reform through proper channels? Wasn't throwing the money changers out of the Temple a far more obstreperous act than occupying a building? But then Jesus was very much a Yippie, which is why he wound up in jail, Jerusalem being the Chicago of its day.

Second, the wielding of the cross exposed a peculiarity of contemporary parent-child relationships. As every movie-goer knows, one carries a cross to ward off vampires, and putting a cross on a door prevents the vampires from getting through. In *The Graduate*, as in upper-middle-class America generally, parents relate to their children in a somewhat vampiresque way. They feed on the child's accomplishments, sucking sustenance for their pale lives from vicarious enjoyment of his or her development. In a sense this sucking is appropriate since the parents give so much—lavish so much care, love, thoughtfulness, and self-sacrifice on their blood bank. But this is little comfort for the child, who at some point must rise above his guilt and live his own life—the culture demands it of him. And after all, a vampire is a vampire.

We are shown this relationship at the very beginning of the film when a party is given to celebrate the hero's return from an honor-laden college career; family and friends clutch and paw him like a valuable artifact. Much of the satire throughout the film centers on this theme, perhaps best exemplified by the pool scene, in which the hero becomes a mannikin on which his father can display his af-

fluence to his friends. The hero's struggle to shed his diving gear—
to disentangle his own motivation from the vicarious aspirations
of his parents—takes up the entire movie.

In this process Mrs. Robinson is a crucial transitional figure. Unlike the parents, she is not a crypto-vampire but an absolutely open
one. She gives nothing whatever and thus induces no guilt. Nor
does she want to derive any vicarious satisfaction from Ben's
achievements. She wants only to feed on his youth and obtain sexual gratification from him. In this relationship—initially an expression of his Oedipal enthralment—Ben can extricate himself from
these familial entanglements, for Mrs. Robinson's cold exploitative-
ness enables his own motivation to separate itself out and became coherent. In shifting his interest to her daughter he moves a step
further—perhaps as far as he is able. It is significant that at the beginning of this new relationship he adopts a very uncharacteristic
mode of behavior—one which resembles Mrs. Robinson's—as if he
were using her cold and distant personality as a lever to establish
his own separateness prior to forming a serious relationship.

The cross, then, is necessary to ward off the elders, whose vampiresque involvement with the hero has been insufficiently exorcised.
The intense new relationship threatens to arouse all of his old sym-
biotic responses, and these must be magically neutralized—much in
the way puberty rites in primitive societies neutralize the young
boy's attachment to his mother.

Before leaving *The Graduate* we should take note of the hostile
reaction of older adults in the society to the cross incident, which
was widely criticized as being "unnecessary" and "in bad taste."
That they should pick up this issue of "taste" and ignore the meaning of the incident exemplifies a characteristic tendency toward ir-
relevance that exasperates their children. In the midst of a dramatic
confrontation between the generations they are distracted by the
unorthodox use of a religious symbol. In the midst of a dramatic
confrontation between blacks and whites they are distracted by a
four-letter word. In the midst of a dramatic confrontation between
those who espouse and those who oppose the Vietnam war, they
are distracted by the long hair of some of the participants.

The young are baffled, amused, and enraged by these bizarre
responses. They alternately view the middle-aged as hopelessly de-

tached from reality and as willfully perverse. What they overlook is the terror. The young are challenging the fundamental premises on which their elders have based their lives, and they are attacking at all of the weakest points. No one likes to admit that they have spent their lives in a foolish, evil, or crazy manner. Furthermore, the elders were always taught to lie about their feelings. They are not likely to say: "You frighten and depress us. We are afraid we have spent our lives in narrow self-aggrandizement, neglecting and brutalizing our neighbors, pursuing useless and trivial artifacts, and creating a joyless environment. It always seemed the right thing to do, but now we are a little unsure, and anyway we wouldn't know how to behave differently." Instead, they suppress their doubts and fears about themselves by refusing to perceive the meaning of the stimulus. When their children cry for peace or social justice they say, "don't talk dirty" or "get a haircut." This is a way of saying, "There is nothing important or disturbing going on here—this is just my child who is mischievous or careless at times—it is just a family affair" ("But Mother, I'm going to jail—I'm a political prisoner.". . . "Well, at least they'll give you a decent haircut"). It is a desperate attempt to view the world as unchanging—to convert the deep social unrest of the day into the blank torpor of suburban life—to translate Watts into *Julia*, Berkeley and Columbia into *Dobie Gillis*, Chicago into *Mayberry*, and Vietnam into *McHale's Navy*.

This is precisely the way the parents of schizophrenic children typically respond to emotional crises of a personal kind. Lidz and his colleagues illustrate this pattern by telling of a patient who, after much struggle and resistance, finally was able to pour out her anguish and bewilderment to her parents and plead for their understanding and help. At the height of her plaintive entreaty her mother "offhandedly turned to one of the psychiatrists, tugged at the waist of her dress and blandly remarked, 'My dress is getting tight. I suppose I should go on a diet.' "[3] The kind of communication pattern that characterizes the families of schizophrenics appears in a number of contemporary dramas, suggesting that it speaks to a much larger social phenomenon. How, for example, can matters so intrinsically trivial as hair length or apparel arouse reactions of such intensity in people who present themselves as the most sane, stable, and effective members of our society? The answer is that two incompatible processes are taking place at once: the elders are expressing anger, while pretending to themselves that the causes of that anger do not exist.

THE SPOCKIAN CHALLENGE

More deeply revealing of the generational issue than *The Graduate* was the odd non-event that followed the arrest of Dr. Spock.* Many people expected that the arrest, on such a basis, of a man who had been doctor, teacher, and adviser to millions of American mothers would cause a torrent of protest. Instead it was met with a profound and malicious silence.

Why did the mothers turn against their benefactor? What was Spock's impact upon American society and why did it try to revenge itself upon him? Since a man does not write a child-rearing manual as successful as this one unless it strikes extremely responsive chords in its readers, it appears that we have found yet another example of Americans raging against the consequences of their own inclinations.

Spock's book reinforced three trends in American family and child-rearing patterns: permissiveness, individualism, and feminine domesticity. The first two are patterns that have been with us for two centuries, but the last is a relatively recent (post-World-War-II) reversal of an older trend in the opposite direction. Curiously enough, it is also the only one about which Spock does not caution against excess, even in his latest edition.

Current popular discussion has centered around permissiveness, but this is due to two misunderstandings. First, it is usually assumed that permissiveness in child-rearing is a recent American development, which is quite clearly not the case. Every generation of Americans since the first landing has imagined itself to be more per-

---

* Spock was arrested through a device that has become increasingly prominent in modern America: the selective enforcement of laws so vague, broad, and universally violated that they enable any law enforcement officer to arrest almost anyone any time he wishes. This is a modern version of the Bill of Attainder, outlawed by our Constitution, but revived, to all intents and purposes, by the convenient chaos of our legal system.

missive than the previous one, while foreign visitors have resolutely refused to recognize any variation in an unremitting stream of American laxity.[4] Second, it would be absurd in any case to blame parental permissiveness on Spock, who places great emphasis on the child's need for parental control and the importance of not letting the child become a tyrant in the home. The areas in which Spock reinforced "permissiveness" had to do not with social behavior, but with such matters as feeding schedules, toilet training, and the like. Even here he did not advance totally new approaches, but merely revived practices current in America and England prior to the middle of the eighteenth century. While I do not wish to minimize the extent to which Spock has become a *symbol* of permissiveness in child-rearing, I think we will learn more about the nature of his impact and the reaction against him by examining the other two variables.

Spock's work epitomizes the old American tradition that every individual is somehow unique. Furthermore, he implicitly endorses a concept that pervades popular American thinking about education—the notion of an individual having a "potential." This potential is seen as innate, partially hidden, gradually unfolding, fluid, and malleable.[5] The parent cannot simply coerce the child into a set uniform pattern of behavior, because it is important, given our achievement ethic, that a child realize his maximum potential, and this means taking into account present, anticipated, or fantasied characteristics of his own. The concept of potential is thus rooted in individualism and achievement ideology. It also serves, however, as a kind of compromise between biological and environmental determinism. The parent is given not clay but some more differentiated substance with which to mold an adult.

In any case, the notion of individual differences, of special unfolding potentialities, is fundamental in Spock, although the latest edition makes a modest effort to stress more universal social demands on the individual. Indeed, it is curious that he talks of the need to instill social consciousness as if this were something that his previous approach failed to do (presumably because he makes no explicit mention of it in earlier editions). Yet the product of child-centered, Spockian child-rearing is the most socially conscious youth America has ever known. This should warn all of us (in-cluding Spock) against the simple assumption that a deliberate push in a given direction will produce the expected outcome.

Spock is nonetheless concerned about what he feels to be our ex-cessive child-centeredness, although he sees no escape from it: "I doubt that Americans will ever want their children's ambitions to be subordinated to the wishes of the family or the needs of our country."[6] He suggests that the children would be happier if they did, and advises parents to stick to whatever principled guns they have. But this hardly balances the general thrust of his work. From the very beginning Spock's book has tended both to encourage Pygmalionesque fantasies in mothers and to stress the complexity of the task of creating a person out of an infant. His good sense, toler-ance, humanity, and uncanny ability to anticipate the anxieties that everyday child-rearing experiences arouse in young mothers helped seduce them into accepting the implicit (and probably unintended) challenge. Underneath all of the qualifications and demurrals, most middle-class, Spock-oriented mothers believe, deep in their hearts, that if they did their job well enough all of their children would be creative, intelligent, kind, generous, happy, brave, spontaneous, and good—each, of course, in his or her own special way.

It is this challenge and this responsibility that have led mothers to accept the third pattern that Spock has reinforced—feminine domesticity. For Spock makes quite explicit, even in his latest edi-tion, his belief that a woman's place is in the home. He lays great emphasis on the importance and the difficulty of the task of child-rearing, and gives it priority over all other possible activities. He suggests government allowances for mothers otherwise compelled to work, on the grounds that it "would save money in the end"—thus implying that only a full-time mother can avoid bringing up a child who is a social problem. He allows reluctantly that "a few mothers, particularly those with professional training" might be so unhappy if they did not work that it would affect the children—the understanding here is that the professional training was a kind of unfortunate accident the effects of which can no longer be undone. The mother must feel "strongly" about it and have an "ideal ar-rangement" for child care. Otherwise Spock tries to induce guilt: "If a mother realizes clearly how vital this kind of care is to a small child, it may make it easier for her to decide that the extra money she might earn, or the satisfaction she might receive from an outside job, is not so important after all."[7]

Although in other respects Spock merely endorses existing cultural patterns—reinforcing them or making them explicit—one could conceivably make a case for his having contributed to the postwar ultradomestication of the American female, since his book was first published in 1946 when it all began. I personally feel that the flight into the home was only a part of a general postwar retreat from the world—a flight that would have occurred even without *Baby and Child Care*. Yet Spock gave it a certain focus, and supported a set of social arrangements which is now yielding both good and bad results. I raise this point because although Spock is as American as apple pie, he has been attacked as if he had introduced some foreign element into the American socialization process. For the most part, he has been a scapegoat for the ambivalence Americans feel about their own society. Only in his emphasis on domesticity did he introduce a broad departure from the past.

American women have always had a reputation for independence (De Tocqueville commented upon it in 1830). The culture as a whole tends to exert a certain pressure for sexual equality, and women in the nineteenth century were not as protected as in Europe (although they were expected to guard their own chastity as vigorously as if men were guarding it for them). In frontier settings they were too important to yield much power or deference to husbands, and among immigrant groups they were often more employable than their husbands. During the present century labor-saving devices reduced the demands of the home to a minimum, education for women increased, women obtained the vote, and contraception undermined the double standard. The direction of events seemed clear.

After World War II, however, a strange phenomenon occurred. Although more women were working than ever before, this was not true for the professions. Despite more women going to college, a smaller percentage were using this education in any way. In short, while single middle-class women were becoming more and more liberated, married middle-class women were embracing a more totally domestic existence than ever before. But how was this achieved? How could educated women devote their entire lives to a task so shrunken? How could they make it fill the day, let alone fill their minds?* To some extent Parkinson's Law ("work expands to fill the time available to complete it") can be relied upon in such situations, especially with the aid of the advertising industry, which continually invents new make-work chores and new standards of domestic perfection. Television also fills many gaps.

But the main factor facilitating the ultradomestication of the middle-class American female was the magnification of the child-rearing role. Child-rearing is not a full-time job at any age in and of itself. In every other society throughout history women have been busy with other tasks, and reared their children as a kind of parallel activity. The idea of devoting the better part of one's day to child care seldom occurred to anyone because few women ever had time for it before, and when they did they usually turned the job over to a servant. Occasionally someone fiercely determined to produce a genius would devote many hours a day trying to teach an infant Greek, or whatever, but these were eccentricities. In our society it is as if every middle-class parent were determined to rear a John Stuart Mill; it turns one a bit queasy to see them walking about with signs on them so their three-year-olds will learn to read, or complaining that their children are not learning enough in nursery school.

This is not to say that child care *cannot* fill a day. There have been many social inventions that have successfully filled the time gaps created by home appliances. The modern suburban home is neither built nor equipped in a manner that allows for the comfortable or healthy management of an eighteen-month-old child. Living in the suburbs also involves the mother in constantly driving her children about from one activity to another. Anyone could add

* Soviet women achieve "equality" by working twice as hard and long as men do, since Russian men are reluctant to engage in domestic chores. The women work a full-time job and then a full-time domestic job, largely unassisted by either men or machines. Middle-class American women, on the other hand, have much more *opportunity* to make this equality real, since (a) their domestic task is much easier, with more labor-saving devices, (b) American middle-class males are not averse to helping out, and (c) they can obtain outside jobs with shorter hours.

to the list of anomalies created by our being a child-oriented society in the face of a technological environment that is essentially child-antagonistic or at least child-alien. One has only to see a village community in which women work and socialize in groups with children playing nearby, also in groups, supervised by the older ones, or by some of the mothers on a haphazardly shared basis, to realize what is awkward about the domestic role in America. Because the American mother is isolated, she can engage in only one of these three activities at a time—with effort, two. Even taken together they hardly constitute a satisfying occupation for a civilized woman.

But the most important factor here is that the American wife has accepted the Spockian challenge. She has been told: "You have the capacity to rear a genius, a masterpiece. Such an activity is the most important thing you can do and should therefore rightfully absorb all of your time and energy." Given such an attitude it is relatively easy to expand child-rearing into a full-time job. For although Spock has many sensible passages about not martyring oneself to one's children ("needless self-sacrifice sours everybody"), the temptation to do so is enormous given the fact that there is so little else. In all the tedium and meaninglessness of her domestic chores this is the only area that is important enough to be worthy of her attention. We are a product-oriented society, and she has been given the opportunity to turn out a really outstanding product.

Unfortunately, however, there really isn't that much she can do to bring about this end. At first the child sleeps most of the time, and later he spends more and more time amusing himself or playing with other children. It is not particularly helpful to waken a sleeping infant, and parents are not very good playmates for older children. The only way she can feel that she is putting a proper amount of effort into the task is by cultivating the child's natural entropic tendencies to make more housework for herself; or by upsetting and then comforting the child so she can flex her nurturant and therapeutic skills. Since she really doesn't know how to create an outstanding adult and perhaps recognizes, deep in some uncorrupted sanctuary of good sense, that the more actively she seeks it the less likely she is to attain it, the only time she will feel she is engaged in her primary task is when she is meeting minor crises. Naturally this produces a great temptation to induce such crises, indirectly and, of course, without conscious intent.

In a prior discussion of this issue, I suggested that the frequent jovial references to the multiplicity of roles played by housewives in our society serve to mask the fact that the housewife is a nobody.[8] Another custom with a similar function is the laughing narration of the events of a particularly chaotic day, in which one minor disaster follows hard upon another, or several occur simultaneously (". . . and there I was, the baby in one hand, the phone and doorbell both ringing . . ."). These sagas are enjoyed because they conceal the fundamental vacuity of the housewife's existence.[9] Saying, "everything happened at once" is an antidote to the knowledge that nothing ever happens, really.

The emotional and intellectual poverty of the housewife's role is nicely expressed in the almost universal complaint: "I get to talking baby talk with no one around all day but the children." There are societies in which the domestic role works, but in those societies the housewife is not isolated. She is either part of a large extended family household in which domestic activities are a communal effort, or participates in a tightly knit village community, or both. The idea of imprisoning each woman alone in a small, self-contained, and architecturally isolating dwelling is a modern invention, dependent upon an advanced technology. In Moslem societies, for example, the wife may be a prisoner but she is at least not in solitary confinement. In our society the housewife may move about freely, but since she has nowhere to go and is not a part of anything anyway her prison needs no walls.

This is in striking contrast to her pre-marital life, if she is a college graduate. In college she is typically embedded in an active group life with constant emotional and intellectual stimulation. College life is in this sense an urban life. Marriage typically eliminates much of this way of life for her, and children deliver the *coup de grâce*. Her only significant relationship tends to be her husband, who, however, is absent most of the day. Most of her social and emotional needs must be satisfied by her children, who are hardly adequate to the task. Furthermore, since she is supposed to be molding them into superior beings she cannot lean too heavily upon them for her own needs, although she is sorely tempted to do so.

This is, in fact, the most vulnerable point in the whole system. Even if the American housewife were not a rather deprived person, it would be the essence of vanity for anyone to assume that an unformed child could tolerate such massive inputs of one person's personality. In most societies the impact of neuroses and defects in the mother's character is diluted by the presence of many other nurturing agents. In middle-class America the mother tends to be not only the exclusive daytime adult contact of the child, but also a contact with a mission to create a near-perfect being. This means that every maternal quirk, every maternal hang-up, and every maternal deprivation will be experienced by the child as heavily amplified noise from which there is no respite.

We know a little bit about the consequences of one aspect of this situation. Societies in which deprived mothers turn to their children for what they cannot obtain from adults tend to produce males who are vain, boastful, aggressive, and skittish toward women. Such males have great fear of losing self-control, of becoming dependent upon women, of weakness. Male gangs often assume great importance.[10]

Now middle-class American males do not, by and large, fit this description, although American foreign policy is deeply rooted in *machismo* philosophies. One of the reasons may be that in the societies that do produce this kind of male there is a strong sexual component in the maternal involvement with the son, resulting from a voluntary or involuntary sexual distance between husband and wife. But although individual American families often show such sexual displacement (the clinical literature is full of them), the American housewife taken as a general type is not a very sexy creature. Indeed, perhaps her major characteristic is that she has been so thoroughly desexualized.

This is no accident. A seductive mother in a family system involving many caretakers has nothing like the impact she has in a society like ours, where she is almost the whole world to the child. The fact that maternal seductiveness is so often associated with male schizophrenia is closely tied to the sexlessness of American housewives as a group. There seems to be some unconscious recognition of the fact that even ordinary feminine seductiveness, given the magnification that motherhood receives in our society, tends to be disorganiz-

70 THE PURSUIT OF LONELINESS

ing to the child. Since the American mother is so omnipresent and intensely committed to her role, she must be defused, as it were. Her desexualization is necessary in order not to add unduly to the already somewhat overwhelming maternal input the child receives.

Let us consider this desexualization further, since it is both a remarkable phenomenon, given the sexual preoccupations of the society as a whole, and rather poorly understood. In many societies a woman is viewed as relatively neuter until she is married—it is at this point that she becomes a full-fledged female, a sexual being. This is especially the case in societies that are strict about premarital sexuality but indifferent toward extramarital affairs. Yet even in societies in which the exact reverse is true, single girls, however promiscuous, are sometimes viewed as merely children playing. In dress, manner, and interpersonal style it is often the married woman alone who is fully sexual.

In our society the exact opposite is true. Stylistically, it is only young unmarried girls who are allowed to be entirely female. Their appearance is given strong sexual emphasis even before there is anything to emphasize, but as soon as they are married they are expected to mute their sexuality somewhat, and when they become mothers this neutralization is carried even further. This means that whatever sexual appeal exists in a malnourished nymphet is made highly explicit, while the kind of mature and full-blown femininity that has excited Europeans for centuries is masked almost beyond recognition. Suburban housewives in particular often affect hard, severe, tight, and rectangular hair and clothing styles. The effect is rather masculine, especially when combined with a bluff, hearty, and sarcastic conversational style, as it so frequently is.

It is tempting to see in this pattern a compensatory process: women cheated of a career express their "masculinity" in the only form left to them. Certainly it seems appropriate to describe as "masculine" a behavioral style which is a transparent imitation of the way men in our society behave in all-male groups, and the hair and clothing style suggests mobilization—a readiness to participate in some vigorous activity outside the home (Chinese peasant women on their way to the factories seem more casually feminine by comparison).

But what is "masculine" and what is "feminine"? Contemporary psychoanalytic literature is full of absurd statements based on the assumption that sex roles in our own society embody biological universals. We know by now, however, that there is virtually nothing in the way of personal characteristics or behavior that is defined in every culture as masculine or feminine. In some societies women are assumed to be stronger, and carry all the heavy burdens. In some societies women are supposed to be impractical and intuitive, in others men are. In most societies women are seen as earthy, men as spiritual, but Victorian England reversed this order. Even within our own society there are odd contradictions: activity is seen as a masculine characteristic, passivity as feminine. Yet men are supposed to move and talk slowly, while women are expected to be birdlike in body movement—constantly moving their hands, using many more facial muscles, talking rapidly. Paradoxically, a man who is too active in the most physical sense of using many muscles from moment to moment is considered "effeminate."

It should be emphasized, then, that when we talk of "masculine" and "feminine" we are referring only to the ways in which these are customarily defined in our culture, and since sex role definitions change from time to time there is ample room for confusion. If women behave in ways that seem imitative of men, we call this masculine, but if customs change, and certain kinds of activities become redefined as appropriate for females are they "masculine" for doing them? One suddenly realizes that we have stumbled upon a powerful weapon for "keeping women in their place." It is really a very old and familiar weapon, used with great effect against minority groups. It begins with a stereotype—"women cannot think logically," for example. If a woman then demonstrates a capacity for logical thought she is stigmatized as "masculine." The same device is used to discourage women from engaging in professional careers.* The ancient Greeks were extremely adept at this device —so much so that they succeeded for over two millennia in distracting attention from the fact that Greek heroes almost never knew

---

* This has a particularly nasty side-effect upon the medical profession. To show that it is really "a man's job" the nurturing, helping aspects must be deemphasized. Thus the recruitment of physicians selectively favors cold, ungiving, exploitative, competitive, and mercenary personality types, with a result familiar to all.

what to do without help or advice from some woman ("with a mind like a man," of course).

Today's black militants are the first minority group clever enough to have invented a solution to this ruse. Instead of trying to escape the black stereotype and become "white," they have in a sense accepted the stereotype and said "black, even in your stereotypical sense, is better than white." Since American society was in danger of being strangulated by its alienation from the body, this meant, as Eldridge Cleaver has so brilliantly shown, that blacks could quite reasonably view themselves as saviors of the whites, helping them rediscover their own roots.[11] This is a lesson from which American women could learn a great deal. The missions are not even that dissimilar, since alienation from the body, from the emotional life, is largely a white male invention.

Consider, for example, the question with which we began this discussion: have suburban matrons adopted a desexualized, "masculine" style because they have been deprived of careers? Many people would object that most women don't *want* careers. I suspect the women themselves would agree, but I also wonder if deep inside they don't feel the kind of puzzled uneasiness that we always experience when obliged to accept a formulation that makes us lose either way. The problem is that "career" is in itself a masculine concept (i.e., designed for males in our society). When we say "career" it connotes a demanding, rigorous, preordained life pattern, to whose goals everything else is ruthlessly subordinated—everything pleasurable, human, emotional, bodily, frivolous. It is a stern, Calvinistic word, which is why it always has a humorous effect when it is applied to occupational patterns of a less puritanical sort. Thus when a man asks a woman if she wants a career, it is intimidating. He is saying, are you willing to suppress half of your being as I am, neglect your family as I do, exploit personal relationships as I do, renounce all personal spontaneity as I do? Naturally, she shudders a bit and shuffles back to the broom closet. She even feels a little sorry for him, and bewails the unkind fate that has forced him against his will to become such a despicable person. The perennial success of this hoax perhaps contributes to the low opinion that men so often have of feminine intelligence (an opinion which, as any teacher knows, is otherwise utterly unfounded).

A more effective (revolutionary, confronting) response would be to admit that a "career," thus defined, is indeed undesirable— that (now that you mention it) it seems like a pernicious activity for *any* human being to engage in, and should be eschewed by both men *and* women. Of course she doesn't want a "career," nor do most humans, with the exception of a few males crazed, by childhood deprivation or Oedipal titillation, with insatiable desires for fame, power, or wealth. What she wants is a meaningful and stimulating activity, excitement, challenge, social satisfactions—all the things that middle-class males get from their jobs whether they are defined as "careers" or not. Rarely is she willing, however, to pay the price that masculine narcissism seduces men into paying in our society. She therefore accepts the definition of herself as the inferior sex, instead of adopting the revolutionary stance of the black militant ("black is beautiful"), and saying: "My unwillingness to sacrifice a host of human values to my personal narcissism and self-aggrandizement makes me the *superior* sex." Such a stance would in fact liberate both sexes: women would be freed from the suffocating stagnation of the artificial domestic role in which they have been imprisoned; men would be liberated from their enslavement to the empty promise (ever receding, always redefined as just out of reach, and unsatisfying even when grasped) of "success." Both could then live in a gratifying present, instead of an illusory future and an ill-remembered past.

This revolutionary response, however, is never made. Women have long been stereotyped as bastions of conservatism—a stereotype which receives considerable empirical support from attitude surveys. Even war, the most absurd and vicious of all the games that men play, has rarely produced a feminine revolt. Despite their antipathy toward it, despite the fact that they play no part in it and cannot control it, that it is most hurtful to them and destroys what they have created, women seldom resist war, and in some societies are more chauvinistic and bloodthirsty than the men. *Lysistrata* was, after all, a man's fantasy.

The reasons for this are complex and varied, but in our society, at least, feminine conservatism, like the domesticity pattern, is part of a role into which women are inducted by men. Having created a technological and social-structural juggernaut by which they are daily buffeted, men tend to use their wives as opiates to soften the impact of the forces they have set into motion against themselves. Consider, for example, the suburban living pattern: husbands go to the city and participate in the twentieth century, while their wives are assigned the hopeless task of trying to act out a rather pathetic bucolic fantasy oriented toward the nineteenth. Men in their jobs must accept change—even welcome it and foster it—however threatening and disruptive it may seem. They do not know how to abstain from colluding daily in their own obsolescence, and they are frightened. Such men tend to make of their wives an island of stability in a sea of change. The wife becomes a kind of memento, like the bit of earth the immigrant brings from the old country and puts under his bed. He subtly encourages her to espouse absurdly old-fashioned views which he then ridicules when he is with his male associates. There is a special tone of good-natured condescension with which married men gathered together discuss the conservatism of their wives, and one senses how elegantly their ambivalence has been apportioned between them ("it's a great opportunity for me but of course the wife doesn't like to move—she has a lot of ties in the community, and of course the children in school and all . . ."). It permits the husband to be far more adaptable and amenable to change than he really feels.

Ultimately, of course, this kind of emotional division of labor tends to backfire, and this case is no exception. Freed from the necessity of confronting his own resistance to change, and having insulated his wife from experiencing the more exciting and enjoyable aspects of such novelty, he tends to become bored with her and somewhat lonely. She is left behind, "outgrown," as William H. Whyte, Jr., puts it.[12]

The domestication and neutralization of the wife is part of the same process. That is, it is important not only that the wife have low stimulus value for her child, but also that she have low stimulus value for her husband. Our society is presently founded on over-stimulation—on the generation of needs and desires which cannot directly be gratified, but which ensure a great deal of striving and buying in an effort to gratify them. Much if not most of this stimulation is sexual—erotic delights are implicitly attached to almost every product that can be bought in America today, at least by adults. The goal of commercial America, therefore, is to maximize sexual stimulation and minimize sexual availability—in this way an infinite number of products can be inserted in the resulting gap. It is the role of the wife to reverse the process for her beleaguered husband—to combine maximum availability with minimum stimulation. This also backfires, of course, since it is a prescription for boredom.

The only real solution for the housewife in this situation is a revolutionary one—to abandon the opiate role and combat the forces that make her opiate role necessary. This is extremely unlikely to occur. On the other hand there is a powerful force for change in the increasingly bizarre contradiction between premarital and marital feminine roles. Women can be expected more and more to resist induction into such a hopelessly unrewarding life style, as cultural alternatives become increasingly available.

I would like to make one further point before moving on to consider the consequences of this constellation. Men, like all dominant groups, have generally been successful in getting women (like other "minority" groups) to accept whatever definition of their essential character has been convenient for men. One of the oldest gambits, for example, has been to maintain that dominance is sex-linked (as indeed it is, in some species). Thus if a woman assumes any other than a submissive pose she is accused of being "unfeminine." This is an ingenious device for maintaining superior status and has been quite successful. On the other hand, males lose considerably by thus hobbling the personalities of their womenfolk. Whenever men have succeeded in convincing their wives that some human response is "unfeminine," they have sought other women who possessed it.

One has only to think of Sophia Loren or Elizabeth Taylor (to name only the most conspicuous examples) to realize that dominance and aggressiveness in women need detract nothing from their sexual attractiveness. On the contrary, women who have been taught too well that aggressiveness is "unladylike" often seem a bit asexual. There is a depth in the human psyche at which all feelings are one, and the disparagement of any contaminates and constricts all. The universality of aggression-release in fertility rituals illustrates this communality.

There is a limit, in any case, to the amount of emotional crippling that can be borne, and as American women (who, after all, have had a long tradition of being defined as spirited) have been inducted more and more into a colorless, ultradomestic role, they have tended to reject submissiveness as a feminine adjunct. This has led to the rather unattractive combination of the strident drudge, an image strongly reinforced by television and other media.

When we realize that the justification for this horror is the welfare of the child, we begin to see why this same child will encounter some resentment when he or she grows up. The child is not really responsible for the bad bargain the parents have made with each other (and with themselves), but he lends moral credit to it. Indeed, "for the children" is a kind of priest's blessing or notary seal given to all bad marital bargains. And since the child is the sanction for the parents' neurotic division of labor, they cannot help but blame him when they begin to suffer from it. Furthermore, as the suffering increases, this sanction tends more and more to be the only force holding them to it. The husband's ambition and the wife's domesticity originally promised their own rewards and did not need to be buttressed by thoughts of the child's future—just as a voluntary and mutually profitable deal between two businessmen does not initially require a written contract. But such a contract binds them if there is a change of heart, at which point one of them might say, "if it weren't for the contract I wouldn't go on with this." Similarly, as ambition and domesticity fail to bring happiness to husband and wife, respectively, both begin to say, "if it weren't for the children I might chuck this and do something more interesting (enjoyable, fulfilling, exciting, relaxing)." One can admit wanting to tear up a contract, however, and one cannot admit wanting to tear up a child. Nor is it easy for the parents to admit their initial error (if indeed they can even comprehend it). This means that the child is not only a scapegoat but a scapegoat that cannot be attacked. The result is a free-floating resentment with a vague tropism toward youth—a resentment with roots in the parents' discontent with their own lives. This condition would seem ideally suited to produce anger toward young people who show tendencies to live (a) differently and (b) more pleasurably than did the parental generation. In the fantasies of adults, at least, there is a very large group of young people—especially those rather sloppily designated as "hippies"—who do both. It is perhaps for this reason that hippies rouse such extravagant rage in their elders.

This is not to say that the parents do not in fact make sacrifices for their children—in a child-oriented society like ours such sacrifices are very considerable. I am trying to explain why these sacrifices are resented. Parents in many societies make severe sacrifices for their children which never cause any hostile reaction later on, largely because the sacrifices "pay off" in some way, or lead to some predictable outcome. In our society parents never know exactly what their sacrifices will lead to, although they have many fantasies about it.

In the recent past, for example, and in working-class families today, parents sacrificed in order to prepare their children to be economically and socially better off than the parents were, and often hated them for fulfilling this goal and leaving the parents behind. Now middle-class parents sacrifice in order to prepare their children to be emotionally better off—more loving, expressive, creative, cooperative, honest[13]—and once again, resent being outdistanced. In both cases the parents feel left out of the triumphs they made possible; and the children feel ashamed of the parents who wanted them to be superior. The parents want their fantasies of vicarious success fulfilled but never seem to recognize that both kinds of success involve a change to a new milieu from which the parents are automatically excluded. The earlier group of parents wanted their children to become rich and respectable and still remain somehow part of the working-class milieu. The later group want their children to be more cultured, less money-grubbing, more spontaneous and creative, yet still somehow willing to remain on the same treadmill with the parents.

SEX AND THE GENERATION GAP

The most striking phenomenon in the current conflict between the generations is that each generation, in different ways, attempts to disallow the sexuality of the other. Many societies attempt to restrict sexual behavior in the young—our society is peculiar only in that it does so in the context of simultaneously maximizing their sexual significance. At the same time, the sexuality of those to whom sexuality is freely allowed is severely deemphasized. As noted earlier, there is a severe dissociation between sexual availability and sexual interest in the norms of the society (a dissociation whose function will be elucidated in the next chapter). The fact that the young no longer adhere to these sexual norms arouses an anger in their elders which probably owes something to the stylistic desexualization which the elders themselves must undergo in our society. Within the nuclear family itself, after all, the older generation holds an almost universal sexual monopoly (this is what the incest taboo means), but in American society this sexuality is masked. Portrayals of the middle-aged in films and television have traditionally catered to the preoccupations of latency-age school children, who cannot imagine their parents having sexual intercourse. This reached some sort of zenith in a recent film on intermarriage (*Guess Who's Coming for Dinner*) in which the tradeoff for accepting interracial sexuality (highly muted) was the fantasy that sexual interest disappears around the age of fifty or sixty anyway. When sexuality in the middle-aged or elderly does occur it is always in a comic context (e.g., *The Producers*).

Parents contribute to this process by denying their own sexuality to their children. In many societies and subcultures children are as aware that their parents copulate as that they eat, and children imitate the act of love long before they are competent to perform it. But in our society parental sexuality is hidden. The reason for this is that while in these more candid societies parental socialization is broad, shallow, and multifunctional, in our society, at least in the middle class, the family is first and foremost an institution for teaching emotional control. Researchers have found that corporation executives are more reluctant to reveal indecision and doubt to their subordinates than any other characteristic—their primary function is, after all, to make decisions. Similarly, parents are more reluctant to reveal sexual impulses to their children than any other characteristic, because their primary function is to control such impulses. It is certainly not simply a matter of the incest taboo, since primitive societies in which parents make little effort to hide their sexuality from their children often have an even more profound horror of incest than does our own.

The importance of the norm becomes clear when it is violated. Young people who are very comfortable with their own sexuality display great uneasiness when confronted with that of their parents or their parents' generation, and Thomas Cottle has shown dramatically the disruptive psychological impact that parental sexual confidences have upon the children.[14] Yet although I agree with Cottle's main point that destruction of the asymmetry of parent-child relationships is pathogenic, I suspect that these sexual revelations are particularly disorienting in our society, in which the parent-child relationship is emotionally overloaded even without them. There are many societies in which revelation of the parents' sexuality as such (that is, without the role reversal of which Cottle speaks) would no more constitute an abandonment of asymmetry than revelation of the parent eating or sleeping or defecating.

One would imagine that in a society like ours, in which parental sexuality is surrounded with so much anxiety and mystery, children would grow up beset with negative sexual attitudes. Yet today's youth appear strikingly liberated from the repressive sexual norms of their parents—not only have they ignored them behaviorally (as their parents often did, albeit clandestinely) but also attitudinally, and apparently without residual guilt. How did this arise? How could such a marked change occur in so short a time and leave so few traces? Changes in sexual mores have been very frequent in Western history, but it usually takes a few generations both to establish and to dissolve a given type of prudery. However hypocritical the parental generation may seem, they obviously feel strongly about the norms themselves and are infuriated by the open and casual manner in which their children disregard them. Given these strong feelings and the degree of internalization of parental values that typifies middle-class socialization, we would expect the children to be just a little defensive, at least in relation to their parents. Yet this does not seem to be the case. It is possible that sexual problems such as impotence and frigidity may be on the increase and that these are guilt-induced, but there are no sound data on which such a statement can be based. Nor does the existence of an ideology of sexual freedom account for the lack of irrational guilt: the two have coexisted for some time.

Yet I think ideology provides the answer to the question, in a rather oblique way. The younger generation has rid itself of its parents' sexual guilt by displacing it into other spheres. Although they violate their parents' sexual norms with relatively little discomfort, one of the striking characteristics of contemporary youth is a kind of diffuse moral absolutism. It is as if every act must have not merely a practical or pleasurable but also a moral foundation. The puritanism of youth displays itself in an inability to act without ideological justification. Every act becomes a moral act. It is this that both requires and enables them to confide in their parents about concerns the initial premises of which the parents reject.

What today's youth seem incapable of is amoral defiance. They cannot assume the responsibility of committing an act that they define as immoral but too pleasurable to forego. The only way this is possible is to make an ideological issue out of it ("it's good for people to get back into their bodies" or "you have to do what you want to do"). They spend a great deal of time trying not to "cop out" in a society whose corruption generates moral dilemmas that compel a hundred cop-outs a day even for the most obsessionally pure radical. And all of this, of course, makes them extremely vulnerable to moral contamination: when confronted with situations in which they took the easy way out they are unusually demoralized. The radicalism of contemporary youth thus derives its emotional energy from guilt more than anger. One reason (there are many others, some quite practical) why compromising liberals are so despised and extreme conservatives sometimes respected is that the greater moral absolutism of the latter, no matter how antithetical in content, strikes a sympathetic chord.

I have suggested that these characteristics, along with parental desexualization and the intensified child-rearing process, all derive from the emphasis the American middle-class family places on the regulation of emotion—in particular, sexual impulses. Why is this function so important? Why is there so much preoccupation in America with sexual stimulation and with the control of sexual gratification? To these questions, so often encountered in passing, we will now devote more prolonged consideration.

4

Putting pleasure to work

Le diable n'est pas clément
C'est là son moindre défaut
"Que faisiez-vous au temps chaud?"
Dit-il a ce vieux diligent.

"Nuit et jour, à tout venant,
Je travaillais, ne vous déplaise."
"Vous travailliez? J'en suis fort aise:
Eh bien! Jouez maintenant."
(WITH APOLOGIES TO LA FONTAINE)

She asked me to stay and she told me to sit anywhere,
So I looked around and I noticed there wasn't a chair.
LENNON AND MC CARTNEY

I can't get no satisfaction.
JAGGER AND RICHARD

A recent study by an English psychologist found that neurotic anxiety was a very good predictor of success and achievement, both at the individual and at the national level,[1] confirming a long-felt suspicion that something sick forms the driving force for our civilization. Freud argued that "culture . . . obtains a great part of the mental energy it needs by subtracting it from sexuality," and saw civilization as an exchange of happiness for security. He felt this process was probably necessary and possibly desirable, but was troubled by it: "One is bound to conclude that the whole thing is not worth the effort and that in the end it can only produce a state of things which no individual will be able to bear."[2]

81

The urgency of this prophecy grows with the level of anxious and irritable desperation in our society. To assess the validity of Freud's argument that civilization is a parasite on man's eroticism becomes an increasingly pressing task, particularly since the few empirical studies available to us all tend to confirm his hypothesis.[3]

There is one aspect of Freud's theory which is contradicted by the existing evidence. Freud argued that society "borrows" from sexuality in order to neutralize human aggressiveness, although the mechanism through which this was supposed to occur was not described. What evidence there is, however, suggests that restrictions on sexual expression, far from neutralizing aggression, tend to arouse it, just as the frustration-aggression hypothesis would lead us to expect.[4] Apparently sexual restrictions have some more direct relation to civilization: a relationship so powerful that increases in aggressiveness can be tolerated as an unfortunate side effect—or at least have been so tolerated until now.

The nature of the relationship seems to have something to do with energy: "civilized" people are usually described as more energetic or restless than their nonliterate counterparts. This does not mean that they *possess* more energy: even given the same diet the correlation will appear. The difference we are concerned with here lies in the *utilization* of energy. There appears to be, in other words, some difference in motivation.

Konrad Lorenz once remarked that in all organisms locomotion is increased by a bad environment. We might then say that sexual restrictions are a way of artificially creating a bad environment, and hence increasing locomotion. Unfortunately we do not know what constitutes a "bad environment" in this sense, nor why it increases locomotion. Presumably a bad environment is one that is not gratifying, and the locomotion is simply a quest for more adequate or complete gratification. This equation between locomotion and lack of gratification makes us think of holding a carrot in front of a donkey, or an animal on a treadmill. In both cases the constant output of energy by the animal depends upon the sought gratification being withheld. Once gratified, the animal would come to a halt, and further locomotion would have to wait upon adequate deprivation.

Fred Cottrell points out that intermittent energy is relatively useless; hence anything that would translate intermittent expenditure into constant expenditure would be highly valuable from a technological viewpoint.[5] For while such a rate of expenditure would be of no value without an adequate food supply and external energy sources to exploit, the latter will also be useless without a high rate of human expenditure. A complex society would not function (unless totally automated, in which case humans would be the slaves and not the masters of it) if founded on a motivational structure like that of the Siriono, who lie in their hammocks until impelled by agonizing hunger to hunt for food (at which time, however, they will demonstrate an energy, strength, and endurance inaccessible to most civilized men).[6] This kind of intermittency was a source of great consternation to early colonial employers, whose work force always melted away on payday until ways were found to chain them through some system of indebtedness.

But there is a dilemma here. If the donkey never eats he will die, but if he does eat he will stop. How can we get a man to work endlessly for a reward which never comes? Obviously we can never avoid intermittency so long as we are dealing with simple bodily satisfactions, which are easily extinguished. It is clear that a man will work hard for food so long as it is scarce. But what about when he has a full belly? In order to ensure a steady output of energy we must create some sort of artificial scarcity, for it is, paradoxically, only through such scarcity that an abiding surplus of energy can be assured.

Sexual desire provides far better raw material for such an enterprise, since it is an impulse that is both powerful and plastic. Its importance in this respect becomes immediately apparent when we realize that in some hypothetical state of nature it is the only form of gratification that is *not* scarce. In fact, it is infinite. This is what people have in mind when they say that sex is the recreation of the poor.

Yet there is no society that does not put restrictions on this resource. Out of an infinite plenty is created a host of artificial scarcities. It would obviously repay us to look into this matter, since we have already observed that although we live in the most affluent society ever known, the sense of deprivation and discomfort that pervades it is also unparalleled.

The idea of placing restrictions on sexuality was a stunning cultural invention, more important than the acquisition of fire. In it man found a source of energy which was limitless and unflagging—one which enabled him to build his empires on earth. By the weird device of making his most plentiful resource scarce he managed, after many millennia, to make most of his scarce ones plentiful. On the negative side, however, men have achieved this miracle by making themselves into donkeys, pursuing an inaccessible carrot. We are very elegantly liveried donkeys, it is true, but donkeys all the same. The popular use of the term "treadmill" to note the institutions through which men make their living expresses our dim awareness of this metamorphosis.

This raises three questions: (1) how did man happen to transform himself into a donkey? (2) what were the mechanisms through which it was achieved? (3) what are the present consequences of his success?

Trying to find historical beginnings is a trivial as well as futile enterprise. Men are always inventing new follies, most of which are luckily stillborn. What we need to explain is why the invention of sexual scarcity was successful, and not only survived but grew. Most likely it began with the imposition of restrictions on one group by another: women by men, or losers by conquerors. Perhaps temporary restrictions in the service of birth control began it, or perhaps it began with the capacity to symbolize. In any case, once begun, it has always had a tendency to ramify, to diffuse itself, for scarcity breeds scarcity just as anger breeds anger. Once the concept exists that there is not enough, people will begin to deprive each other of what there is.[7]

What sustained this folly was natural selection. Restless, deprived-feeling tribes had a tendency either to conquer their more contented neighbors or more fully to exploit the resources around them, or both. This cultural superiority was by no means automatic, of course. Without the right kind of environment this restlessness was merely destructive, and many of the institutions that have evolved from various scarcity mechanisms are so cumbersome and costly that they absorb more energy than the scarcity mechanism makes available. The ethnographic literature contains as many societies of this type as it does societies that are simply culturally marginal.[8] But from time to time scarcity mechanisms have combined with appropriate economic and ecological conditions to produce societies so "successful" in a competitive sense that the planet has become increasingly peopled with rich scarcity-oriented societies. Occasionally such societies have had their sense of deprivation eroded by luxury, and the cultures they have created have been taken over and continued by "less effete," "more virile" (i.e., more deprived-feeling) societies, which contributes further to the selection process.

The mechanisms through which sexual scarcity is created are many and complex, and it should be emphasized strongly that we are not discussing anything as simple as frequency of sexual intercourse or orgasm (although there is growing evidence that these, too, are negatively related to civilization).[9] A man may have intercourse as often as he wishes and still feel deprived, because his desire has attached itself to someone or something unattainable. The root of sexual dissatisfaction is the capacity of man to generate symbols which can attract and trap portions of his libido. Restrictions as to time, place, mode, and partner do not simply postpone release but create an absolute deprivation, because man has the capacity to construct a memory, a concept, a fantasy. Thus while increases in the number, variety, and severity of sexual restrictions may intensify the subjective experience of sexual scarcity, a subsequent trend toward sexual "permissiveness" need not produce a corresponding decrease in scarcity. Once you have trained your dog to prefer cooked meat you can let him run about the stockyard without any qualms. The fundamental mechanism for generating sexual scarcity is to attach sexual interest to inaccessible, nonexistent, or irrelevant objects; and for this purpose man's capacity to symbolize is perfectly designed.

Today this basic technique has become the dominant one. By the time an American boy or girl reaches maturity he or she has so much symbolic baggage attached to the sexual impulse that the mere mutual stimulation of two human bodies seems almost meaningless. Through the mass media everything sexless has been sexualized: automobiles, cigarettes, detergents, clothing. (A recent TV commercial showed a lovesick man donning, with many caresses, and to the accompaniment of "I'm in the Mood for Love," a pair of shoes.) The setting and interpretation of a sexual act come to hold more excitement than the act itself.

Thus although the Soviet Union is probably more overtly puritanical than the U.S., there is far more manipulation of the sexual impulse here. Russians are not daily bombarded with bizarre sexual stimuli and deranged erotic associations, so that their simple restrictions are ultimately far less repressive.

Romantic love is one scarcity mechanism that deserves special comment. Indeed, its only function and meaning is to transmute that which is plentiful into that which is in short supply. This is done in two ways: first, by inculcating the belief that only one object can satisfy a person's erotic and affectional desires; and second, by fostering a preference for unconsummated, unrequited, interrupted, or otherwise tragic relationships. Although romantic love always verges on the ridiculous (we would find it comic if a man died of starvation because he could not obtain any brussels sprouts) Western peoples generally and Americans in particular have shown an impressive tendency to take it seriously. Why is this so? Why is love made into an artificially scarce commodity, like diamonds, or "genuine" pearls (cf. "true" love)?

To ask such a question is to answer it. We make things scarce in order to increase their value, which in turn makes people work harder for them. Who would spend their lives working for pleasures that could be obtained any time? Who would work for love, when people give it away? But if we were to make some form of it somehow rare, unattainable, and elusive, and to devalue all other forms, we might conceivably inveigle a few rubes to chase after it.

This does not in itself, however, account for the wide diffusion of romantic love. To see its function is not to explain its existence. We can only assume that it derives its strength from some intense emotional experience. Few primitive peoples are familiar with it, and in general it seems to be most highly developed in those cultures in which the parent-child relationship is most exclusive (as opposed to those in which the child-rearing role is diffused among so many people as to approach the communal).

Since romantic love thrives on the absence of prolonged contact with its object one is forced to conclude that it is fundamentally unrelated to the character of the love object, but derives its meaning

from prior experience. "Love at first sight" can only be transfer-
ence, in the psychoanalytic sense, since there is nothing else on
which it can be based. Romantic love, in other words, is Oedipal
love. It looks backwards, hence its preoccupation with themes of
nostalgia and loss. It is fundamentally incestuous, hence its emphasis on obstacles and nonfulfillment, on tragedy and trespass.[10] Its
real object is not the actual parent, however, but a fantasy image of
that parent which has been retained, ageless and unchanging, in the
unconscious.

Romantic love is rare in primitive communities simply because
the bond between child and parent is more casual. The child tends
to have many caretakers and be sensitive to the fact that there exist many alternative suppliers of love. The modern Western child,
brought up in a small detached household does not share this sense
of substitutability. His emotional life is heavily bound up in a single
person, and the process of spreading this involvement over other
people as he grows up is more problematic. Americans must make
a life task out of what happens effortlessly (insofar as it need happen at all) in many societies. Most Western children succeed in
drawing enough money out of their emotional bank to live on, but
some always remain tied up in Oedipal fantasy. Most of us learn
early that there is one relationship that is more vital than all the
others put together, and we tend both to reproduce this framework
in later life and to retain, in fantasy, the original loyalty.

The underlying scarcity mechanism on which romantic love is
based is thus the intensification of the parent-child relationship. It
creates scarcity by a) inculcating a pattern of concentrating one's
search for love onto a single object, and b) focusing one's erotic
interest on an object with whom consummation is forbidden. The
magnification of the emotionality and exclusiveness of the parent-
child bond, combined with the incest taboo, is the prototypical
scarcity mechanism.

We can think of this process as a kind of forced savings (indeed,
emotional banking was probably the unconscious model for the
monetary form). The more we can bind up an individual's erotic
involvement in a restricted relationship the less he will seek pleasure
in those forms that are readily available. He will consume little and
produce much. Savings will increase, profits will be reinvested. So

long as he is pursuing what cannot be captured we can relax in the assurance that he will work without cessation into the grave. We have found our donkey.

I observed earlier that bodily gratification is easily obtained, and that in order to motivate people to strive on a continuous basis we must intrude restrictions or symbolic definitions which will block or filter this gratification and render it incomplete. Hunger, thirst, and sexual desire in pure form can be slaked, but the desire for a body type that never existed but was invented by cartoonists cannot be slaked. Neither can the desire for fame, power, or wealth as such. These are inherently invidious needs; they are satisfied only in relation to the deprivation of others. Furthermore they are purely symbolic and hence have no logical consummation. A man hooked on fame or power will never stop striving because there is no way to gratify a desire with a symbol. One cannot eat, drink, or copulate with a Nobel Prize, a presidency, or a controlling interest. One can purchase bodily gratifications by virtue of these achievements, of course, but they can also be obtained without such striving. In any case, they typically play a secondary role in the emotional lives of those engaged in such pursuits—serving as a vacation from or an aid to further productivity.

When we ask why men *do* pursue fame, power, and unlimited wealth so assiduously the answer is usually that these have become ends in themselves. This is in a sense true, but it does not answer the question, since the goals have no intrinsic worth. When a means is not used for an end, but becomes an end, then we must assume that the end has been lost or forgotten. We may have stopped using the carrot, but somewhere in the back of the donkey's head it still exists. He does not trot merely because he has come to enjoy the exercise.

When we say of such a man that he is "married to his job" we betray our unconscious understanding of the motivational roots of his striving. Men who pursue these ephemeral goals are those with most of their emotional funds tied up in the maternal bank. They have a little spending money for daily pleasures but they are not satisfied with ordinary love. They are committed to an Oedipal fantasy—an emotional long shot that will never pay off. They will work their lives away to achieve a love that is unattainable. They cannot amass enough wealth to buy it, obtain enough power to command it, achieve enough fame to attract it, or do enough good works to deserve it, but still they try. Such men are the most successfully metamorphosed of all.*

It is by becoming a donkey that social mobility is achieved. The first class system that every individual encounters is the division between adult and child, and the complex distribution of prerogatives, compensations, dependencies, and freedoms that goes with it. The little boy knows that to replace his father altogether in his mother's affections he must move out of the child class and into the adult class, but by the time this happens the whole fantasy has usually been relegated to the attic of childhood memories. Yet if the son is in subtle ways encouraged by the mother, because of the father's inadequacies as a provider, or because of special ambitions of her own, he will work out his Oedipal strivings on a socioeconomic stage. It is this Oedipal fantasy, in fact, that sustains the upwardly mobile individual as he ruthlessly cuts away all the mundane community bonds and loyalties that threaten to hold him down. And it is the value we place on this fantasy game that has made us as a nation so rootless, so community-poor, and so sentimental about motherhood.

Another outcome of this process is an increase in human destructiveness. Man may have transformed himself into a donkey, but it is a very irritable donkey. Cross-culturally there is a correlation between the degree to which a society places restrictions on bodily pleasure—particularly in childhood—and the degree to which the

---

* It is ironic that in the latest edition of his book (pp. 14–16) Spock makes explicit and approving recognition of many aspects of this process, the consequences of which he has fought so bitterly.

I have used the terms "parent" and "mother" more or less interchangeably here, since the discussion primarily concerns male children. The relationship with the mother is of course the primary one for both sexes and this has important consequences for feminine striving. Ambitious women tend to have the same kind of intense involvement with their fathers that ambitious men have with their mothers—an attachment that is more often openly acknowledged. But the fact that affectional involvement tends for females to be more evenly divided between the parents is perhaps the source of their lesser willingness to invest in a "career." This is also why women are in a better position to liberate our society emotionally.

society engages in the glorification of warfare and sadistic practices.[11]

Nuclear war holds an unconscious attraction because it offers a final explosive release from the tensions that afflict us, and aggression in less extreme forms provides a similar outlet. But war also plays a practical role in maintaining the donkey-carrot syndrome. Our society has become so affluent that it threatens to give the show away—to disclose the absurdity of the scarcity assumptions on which it is based. War creates an artificial scarcity in the economic sphere and thus adds, as it were, another set of blinders to the donkey's equipment, lest he notice that carrots grow in abundance along the roadside. It is grotesque, for example, that any major service institution in a society as wealthy as ours should experience a financial crisis—what is our wealth good for if it does not provide these services? Yet in fact all of them—schools, hospitals, universities, local governments, pure science, the arts—are enmeshed in such crises. War maintains, justifies, and explains these anomalies, although it did not create them.

The past decade, however, has also seen the emergence of a significant counterculture. Although it takes many different forms, the emphasis on recapturing direct, immediate, and uncontaminated bodily and sensory experience is common to all. I shall explore the relationship between this counterculture and the husk in which it is embedded in the next chapter. Here I would like merely to examine the reaction of the older culture to it, as a way of further revealing the mechanism we have been discussing.

One of the most automatic responses of older people to the more casual sexuality, the clothing styles, and the use of drugs among the young is to ask "what is it *for?*" Sometimes various utilitarian motives are imputed: the clothes are to attract attention, the sexual freedom is designed to produce a better marriage (the term "sexual experimentation" captures this utilitarian assumption nicely), the drugs are to "test" oneself. The idea that pleasure could be an end in itself is so startling and so threatening to the structure of our society that the mere possibility is denied.

In our society pleasure is allowable only as a means to an end which is itself a mere means. It must in some way or another yield energy for the economy. Thus direct sexual gratification is attacked, but symbolic sexual stimulation, in such attenuated forms as *Playboy*, is acceptable. The attempt to gain simple, direct gratification in personal ways is punished more severely than robbing and swindling one's neighbor, which maintains the energy flow. Our society has developed a number of secondary scarcity mechanisms to enforce this priority. Pleasure is made scarce, for example, by making it illegal. This makes it expensive and more difficult to obtain, and forces people to compete for what would otherwise be plentiful. Making liquor, drugs, prostitution, pornography, or gambling illegal also opens up new career pathways for the aggressive and ruthless.

Indeed, utilitarian assumptions even control our attitudes toward idleness. In public places one is suspect and at times subject to arrest if he is not engaged in at least a minimal activity—going or coming, fishing, "getting a tan," reading the paper, smoking, "window shopping." One must always be able to make a case for every action having some vague utilitarian value—"broadening the outlook," "keeping up," "making contact," "keeping in shape," "taking the mind off work for a bit," "getting some relaxation."[12] The answer to "what are you doing?" can be "nothing" only if one is a child. An adult's answer must always imply some ulterior purpose—something that will be fed back into the mindless and unremitting productivity of the larger system.

This utilitarian emphasis also underlies current American attitudes toward pornography and drugs. In both cases there is a condemnation of that which is everywhere and on the increase. In both cases the society fosters the processes that produce that which is condemned. And in both cases the condemned phenomena threaten the instrumentalization of sexuality by a kind of circuit overload.

If we define pornography as any message from any communication medium that is intended to arouse sexual excitement, then it is clear that most advertisements are covertly pornographic. But when we examine the specific rules concerning what is or is not allowed in various contexts we discover that the real issue is one of completion: the body can be only partially nude, sexual organs cannot be shown, a sexual act cannot be completed, and so on. The reason for this is that a partial or minimal arousal can be harnessed for instrumental purposes, while too strong an impulse will distract the audience from these purposes—will lead them to forsake buying for orgasm.

This leads to a self-defeating cycle. The more successful we are in getting ourselves to substitute products for real satisfactions—in generating esoteric erotic itches that cannot be scratched outside the world of fantasy, but lend themselves well to marketing—the stronger becomes the desire to obtain pure and uncontaminated gratifications. Our senses are numbed by utility, and the past decade has seen an impressive flowering of techniques and movements and exhortations designed to reverse this process. Now, the more attractive the idea of uncontaminated experience becomes, the closer must all media approximate it before pulling back and shunting the audience off into the market place. But raising the ante in this way simply aggravates the need, and the whole process can only escalate until the donkey either gets his carrot or runs amok. The "relaxation" of restrictions on sexual material in all media is not a relaxation at all, but merely another intensification of the control-release dialectic on which Western civilization is so unfortunately based.

Critics of censorship are fond of pointing out that censors are strangely tolerant of violence—that it is perfectly all right for a man to shoot, knife, strangle, beat, or kick a woman so long as he doesn't make love to her. An irate father taking his children to a "family movie" (consisting of brutal killings and the glorification of violence and hatred) complained bitterly when they were exposed to previews that showed some bare flesh and lovemaking. The children must be trained into our competitive value system, in which it is moral for people to hurt one another and immoral for them to give pleasure to one another.

Lenny Bruce used to point out that a naked body was permissible in the mass media as long as it was mutilated. This is true, but for a very good reason: our society needs killers from time to time—it does not need lovers. It depends heavily upon its population being angry and discontented; the renunciation of violence would endanger our society as we now know it. Failure to do so, of course, endangers its human participants, but our society was not designed for people. The reason a mutilated body is more acceptable than a whole one is that it is only in mutilated form that the sexual impulse can exist in America. In pure form it would dissolve our culture and consign its machinery to rust and ruin, leaving a lot of embarrassed people alone with each other.

The same dialectic is involved in the case of drugs. Pot and LSD promise a return to pure experience, to unencumbered sensation. Their devotees want to encounter the world in terms of what it is rather than how it can be used . . . ("this beach will be a valuable resort property some day"). They want to stop using themselves as machines.

Yet the means they employ to achieve this end involve just that. For drugs, like "pornography," are both a logical development from, and a reaction against, our culture. They are attacked for being insufficiently partial—they blow the mind instead of just tickling it. Yet in the last analysis they merely raise the ante, and the temptation of the market place to incorporate and exploit them grows daily.

For fundamentally, drug users are behaving like good American consumers. The mass media tell us continually to satisfy our emotional needs with material products—particularly those involving oral consumption of some kind. Our economy depends upon our willingness to turn to things rather than people for gratification—to symbols rather than our bodies. The gross national product will reach its highest point when a material object can be interpolated between every itch and its scratch.

Training in this regard begins even before television. Mothers are always advised that if their two-year-old masturbates they should take his hand away and give him a toy, and most parents would prefer to have their child sucking a pacifier rather than a thumb, and clutching a blanket rather than a penis.

The drug world simply extends this process in its effort to reverse it. If the body can be used as a working machine, and a consuming machine, why not an experience machine? The drug user makes precisely the same assumption as do other Americans—that the body is some sort of appliance. Hence they must "turn on" and "tune in" in their unsuccessful effort to drop out. They may be enjoying the current more, but they are still plugged into the same machinery that drives other Americans on their weary and joyless round.

These examples should explain why the mass media in our society seem so omnivorous—devouring and trivializing each new bud of change almost before it can fully emerge. It was this insatiable need to make every eccentric effusion familiar to all that evoked Marcuse's despair in *One-Dimensional Man*. I am always reminded of those science-fiction monsters that "eat" radioactivity and must constantly seek new sources of this energy. What the mass media eat is new forms of emotional expression. The more the sexual impulse is exploited instrumentally the more "valuable" it becomes economically. The act of buying has become so sexualized in our society that packaging has become a major industry: we must even wrap a small purchase before carrying it from the store to our home. Carrying naked purchases down the street in broad daylight seems indecent to Americans (Europeans can still do it but are becoming increasingly uneasy as advertising in Europe becomes more sexualized). After all, if we are induced to buy something because of the erotic delights that are covertly promised with it, then buying becomes a sexual act. Indeed we are approaching the point where it absorbs more sexual interest than sex itself; when this happens people will be more comfortable walking in the street nude than with an unwrapped purchase. Package modesty has increased in direct proportion as body modesty has lessened.

But sexuality as a marketing resource is not inexhaustible. In the absence of real gratification interest threatens to flag, and the search for new raw material is an increasingly desperate one. New images, new fantasies of an exciting, adventurous, and gratifying life must be activated. Efforts to reverse the direction of the society are gobbled up to further titillate and excite the product-filled discontent that prevails.

Eldridge Cleaver has promised that blacks will rescue America from all this by a kind of emotional transfusion. While Freud called man "a kind of prosthetic God" whose auxiliary organs had not quite grown onto him yet, Cleaver suggests that today the reverse is true—that man needs "an affirmation of his biology" and "a clear definition of where his body ends and the machine begins." He argues that "blacks, personifying the Body and being thereby in closer communion with their biological roots than other Americans," can provide this affirmation—can clarify and rationalize the boundary between man and the extensions of man.[13]

How much this needs to be done becomes apparent when one listens to Western employers in developing nations complaining that their workers have not learned "rational" Western attitudes toward machinery. Upon probing further one discovers that these "rational" attitudes consist in (a) acting as if one owned the machine, and (b) treating it as a person. Our Western view is apparently that animism is rational when it pertains to inanimate man-made objects but irrational and "primitive" when it pertains to animate ones. If non-Western workers need more libidinal involvement with machines, it seems very clear that Americans could do with less of it, and Cleaver may well be correct in arguing that blacks can teach us this. It may even be that white involvement in civil rights began in response to some dim awareness of deficiencies in our culture—an awareness that whites needed to learn something from blacks about how to live.

In other words, blacks, being imagined to have a more pure, less warped and contaminated libidinal existence, are seen—very ambivalently, to be sure—as a source of revitalization for the total society. But once again, there are two ways of viewing this process —just as there were in the case of "relaxed" sexual norms, drugs, and the hippie movement. Is it revolutionary, a new and saving force? Or is it merely more libidinal raw material in the process of being gobbled up by the ravenous science-fiction monster on which our society rests? Is it not possible that drugs, blacks, and hippies will all end as sources of additional sensual titillation, designed to inflame Americans into further frantic buying and demented striving? Will they free the donkey or just provide a more exotic carrot? Can they rescue Americans, as Isis rescued Lucius, from their dreams and their machines?

5

Half slave, half free

We shall be able to rid ourselves of many of the pseudo-moral principles which have hag-ridden us for two hundred years, by which we have exalted some of the most distasteful of human qualities into the position of the highest virtues.
KEYNES

Consider the lilies of the field, how they grow; they toil not, neither do they spin: and yet I say unto you, that even Solomon in all his glory was not arrayed like one of these.
MATTHEW 6:28–29

Don't you know that it's a fool
Who plays it cool
By making his world a little colder.
LENNON AND MC CARTNEY

And what's the point of revolution
Without general copulation.
WEISS

In the new there is always an admixture of the old, and this is true of the protean counterculture now burgeoning in the United States. This makes it very difficult, as we saw in the last chapter, to tell what is a true counterculture and what is simply a recruiting outpost for the old culture. But the mere fact that the old culture tries to gobble up something new does not invalidate the potential revolutionary impact of this novelty. At some point a devourer always

96

overreaches himself, like the witch or giant in folk tales who tries to drink up the sea and bursts, or like the vacuum monster in *Yellow Submarine* who ultimately devours himself and disappears. This seems to me the most probable future for the old culture in America.

When I talk of two separate cultures in America I do not mean rich and poor, or black and white (or science and humanism), but rather the opposition between the old scarcity-oriented technological culture that still predominates and the somewhat amorphous counterculture that is growing up to challenge it. At times this distinction may seem synonymous with old-versus-young, or radical-versus-conservative, but the overlap is only approximate. There are many young people who are dedicated to the old culture and a few old people attracted to the new; while as to politics, nothing could be more old-culture than a traditional Marxist.

I speak of two cultures, first because each is in fact a total system with an internal logic and consistency: each is built upon a set of assumptions which hangs together and is viable under some conditions. Second, I wish to emphasize a fact which has escaped the liberal-centrist group that plays so dominant a role in America: that they are no longer being wooed so fervently by those to the left and right of them. The seduction of the center is a phenomenon that occurs only in societies fundamentally united. This has in the past been true of the United States and most parliamentary democracies, but it is true no longer. I speak of two cultures because we no longer have one. Mixing the two that exist does not add up to the American way of life. They cannot be mixed. From two opposing systems—each tightly defined—can only come a collision and a confusion. No meaningful compromise can be found if the culture as a whole is not articulated in a coherent way. American centrists—liberal university presidents are the best example—are still operating under the illusion that all Americans are playing by the same rules, an assumption which puts the centrists into the advantageous position of mediators. But this is not the case. Indeed, the moderates are increasingly despised by both radicals and conservatives as hypocritical, amoral, and opportunistic—people who will take no stand and are only interested in their own careers.

What we see instead are two growing absolutistic groups with a shrinking liberal one in between, a condition that will probably obtain until some new cultural structure emerges which is more widely shared. The left attacks the middle most vigorously, since its equivocating stances and lack of conviction make it morally the most vulnerable. Times of change are times when the center is crushed in this way—when it is regarded as the least rather than the most valid, when it is an object of contempt rather than a court of appeal. As the new culture settles in, a new center will grow in strength—become dominant and sure, acquire moral conviction.

So long as our society had a common point of moral reference there was a tendency for conflicts to be resolved by compromise, and this compromise had a moral as well as practical basis. Today this moral unity is gone, and the *only* basis for compromise is a practical one. Whenever moral sentiments are aroused, the opposing groups are pulled in opposite directions, and mere expedience is usually too weak a consideration to counteract this divergence.

For the older generation, the ultimate moral reference group is the far right—authoritarian, puritanical, punitive, fundamentalist. Such views are of course considered extreme, impractical, and "moralistic," but they are accorded an implicit and unquestioned *moral* validity. The liberal majority generally feel uncomfortable and awkward defining issues in moral terms, but when it becomes inescapable it is this brand of morality that they tend to fall back upon. They are practical and "realistic" as long as possible, but when accused of moral flabbiness or being too compromising they feel called upon to pay homage to a kind of Bible Belt morality. They tend to view their position as one of sensible men mediating between hypermoralistic conservatives and amoral radicals, bending the rigid rules of the former to accommodate and indulge the latter.

For middle-class college students the ultimate moral reference group tends increasingly to be the New Left, with its emphasis on equalitarianism, radical democracy, social justice, and social commitment. Once again the moderate majority among the young tend to view the proponents of their moral code as extreme, moralistic, and fanatic. They regard the militant activists as pursuing a course which is too pure and demanding to be realistic. Allowances must be made for human frailty—the narcissistic needs of those in power, resistance to change, and so on. They, too, see themselves as mediating, but this time between hypermoralistic radicals and amoral conservatives.

So long as the two sides do not feel that a significant moral issue is at stake they can reach a compromise, and the illusion of a unitary culture can be maintained. But sooner or later a moral issue *is* at stake, and negotiations then break down. This is because each side feels it has to justify itself to its moral reference group—to prove that it is not merely giving in out of weakness and cowardice— to prove that it is willing to stand up for some principle. But instead of being common principles, shared by the vast central majority of the society, with each side attempting to show that they are closer to this central morality, the principles are at opposite poles, pulling the sides apart. Today expedience is the *only* unifying force in campus confrontations; no morally based unity is possible.

This may have something to do with the peculiar obtuseness that seems to afflict college presidents, who appear to learn nothing from each other's mistakes or even their own. They are unwilling to face the absence of an even minimal value consensus and keep trying to manufacture one ("the preservation of the university," "the maintenance of free expression and rational discourse," etc.). They talk of "outside agitators" and "a small disruptive minority" and, acting on their own rhetoric, soon find themselves confronted with a hostile majority. They shrink from facing the fact that an ever increasing number of students (for despite the deliberate attempts of admissions officers to prevent it, each entering class is more radical than the last) reject the legitimacy of the established order. The legal monopoly of violence is being challenged by students—they see the crimes of "legitimate" order as demanding extra-legal countermeasures: "An opposition which is directed . . . against a given social system as a whole, cannot remain legal and lawful because it is the established legality and the established law which it opposes." Since the crimes of the society are defended and protected by legal techniques they can only be attacked by extra-legal means. Since the forces of law and order fail to comply with their own standards their "betrayed promises are, as it were, 'taken over' by the opposition, and with them the claim for legitimacy."[1]

What all this means is that the university is no longer one society with shared norms of proper behavior, fair play, tolerance and so on, as university administrators try to pretend. Students are not simply challenging an authority they fundamentally accept. Campus confrontations are warfare, with neither side accepting the validity of occupation and control by the other. Students who take over a building hold the same view of this act as police do of wiretapping: the enemy is too dangerous to give them the benefit of the doubt; their crimes require emergency measures.

THE OLD CULTURE AND THE NEW

There are an almost infinite number of polarities by means of which one can differentiate between the two cultures. The old culture, when forced to choose, tends to give preference to property rights over personal rights, technological requirements over human needs, competition over cooperation, violence over sexuality, concentration over distribution, the producer over the consumer, means over ends, secrecy over openness, social forms over personal expression, striving over gratification, Oedipal love over communal love, and so on. The new counterculture tends to reverse all of these priorities.

Now it is important to recognize that these differences cannot be resolved by some sort of compromise or "golden mean" position. Every cultural system is a dynamic whole, resting on processes that must be accelerative to be self-sustaining. Change must therefore affect the motivational roots of a society or it is not change at all. An attempt to introduce some isolated element into such a system produces cultural redefinition and absorption of the novel element if the culture is strong, and deculturation if it is susceptible. As Margaret Mead points out, to introduce cloth garments into a grass- or bark-clad population, without simultaneously introducing closets, soap, sewing, and furniture, merely transforms a neat and attractive tribe into a dirty and slovenly one. Cloth is part of a complex cultural pattern that includes storing, cleaning, mending, and protecting—just as the automobile is part of a system that includes fueling, maintenance, and repair. A fish with the lungs of a land mammal still will not survive out of water.

Imagine, for example, that we are cooperation purists attempting to remove the invidious element from a foot race. We decide, first of all, that we will award no prize to the winner, or else prizes to everyone. This, we discover, brings no reduction in competitiveness. Spectators and participants alike are still preoccupied with who won and how fast he ran relative to someone else now or in the past. We then decide to eliminate even *announcing* the winner. To our dismay we discover that our efforts have generated some new cultural forms: the runners have taken to wearing more conspicuous identifying clothing—bright-colored trunks or shirts, or names emblazoned in iridescent letters—and underground printed programs have appeared with names, physical descriptions, and other information facilitating this identification. In despair we decide to have the runners run one at a time and we keep no time records. But now we find that the sale of stopwatches has become a booming enterprise, that the underground printed programs have expanded to include voluminous statistics on past time records of participants, and that private "timing services," comparable to the rating services of the television industry, have grown up to provide definitive and instantaneous results for spectators willing to pay a nominal sum (thus does artificial deprivation facilitate enterprise).

At this point we are obliged to eliminate the start and finish lines —an innovation which arouses angry protest from both spectators and participants, who have evinced only mild grumbling over our previous efforts. "What kind of a race can it be if people begin and end wherever they like? Who will be interested in it?" To mollify their complaints and combat dwindling attendance, we reintroduce the practice of having everyone run at the same time. Before long we observe that the runners have evolved the practice of all starting to run at about the same time (although we disallow beginning at the same place), and that all of the races are being run on the circular track. The races get longer and longer, and the underground printed programs now record statistics on how many laps were run by a given runner in a given race. All races have now become longevity contests, and one goes to them equipped with a picnic basket. The newer fields, in fact, do not have bleachers, but only tables at which drinks are served, with scattered observation windows through which the curious look from time to time and report to their tables the latest news on which runners are still going. Time passes, and we are increasingly subjected to newspaper attacks concerning the corrupt state into which our efforts have fallen. With great trepidation, and in the face of enormous opposition from the ideologically apathetic masses, we inaugurate a cultural revolution and make further drastic alterations in racing rules. Runners begin and end at a signal, but there is no track, merely an open field. A runner must change direction every thirty seconds, and if he runs parallel with another runner for more than fifteen seconds he is disqualified. At first attendance falls off badly, but after a time spectators become interested in how many runners can survive a thirty-minute race without being eliminated for a breach of these rules. Soon specific groups become so skilled at not running parallel that none of them are ever disqualified. In the meantime they begin to run a little more slowly and to elaborate intricate patterns of synchronizing their direction changes. The more gifted groups become virtuosi at moving parallel until the last split second and then diverging. The thirty-second rule becomes unnecessary as direction changes are voluntarily frequent, but the fifteen-second rule becomes a five-second one. The motions of the runners become more and more elegant, and a vast outpouring of books and articles descends from and upon the university (ever a dirty bird) to establish definitive distinctions between the race and the dance.

The first half of this parable is a reasonably accurate representation of what most liberal reform amounts to: opportunities for the existing system to flex its muscles and exercise its self-maintaining capabilities. Poverty programs put very little money into the hands of the poor because middle-class hands are so much more gifted at grasping money—they know better where it is, how to apply for it, how to divert it, how to concentrate it. That is what being middle class means, just as a race means competition. No matter how much we try to change things it somehow ends as merely a more complex, intricate, bizarre, and interesting version of what existed before. A heavily graduated income tax somehow ends by making the rich richer and the poor poorer. "Highway beautification" somehow turns into rural blight, and so on.

But there is a limit to the amount of change a system can absorb, and the second half of the parable suggests that if we persist in our efforts and finally attack the system at its motivational roots we may indeed be successful. In any case there is no such thing as "compromise": we are either strong enough to lever the train onto a new track or it stays on the old one or it is derailed.

Thus it becomes important to discern the core motivational logic behind the old and the new cultures. Knowing this would make rational change possible—would unlock the door that leads most directly from the old to the new.* For a prolonged, unplanned collision will nullify both cultures, like bright pigments combining into gray. The transition must be as deft as possible if we are to minimize the destructive chaos that inevitably accompanies significant cultural transformations.

The core of the old culture is scarcity. Everything in it rests upon the assumption that the world does not contain the wherewithal to satisfy the needs of its human inhabitants. From this it follows that people must compete with one another for these scarce resources—lie, swindle, steal, and kill, if necessary. These basic assumptions create the danger of a "war of all against all" and must be buttressed by a series of counternorms which attempt to qualify and restrain the intensity of the struggle. Those who can take the largest share of the scarce resources are said to be "successful," and if they can do it without violating the counternorms they are said to have character and moral fibre.

The key flaw in the old culture is, of course, the fact that the scarcity is spurious—man-made in the case of bodily gratifications and man-allowed or man-maintained in the case of material goods. It now exists only for the purpose of maintaining the system that depends upon it, and its artificiality becomes more palpable each day. Americans continually find themselves in the position of having killed someone to avoid sharing a meal which turns out to be too large to eat alone.

The new culture is based on the assumption that important human

* This of course makes the assumption that some kind of drastic change is either desirable or inevitable. I do not believe our society can long continue on its old premises without destroying itself and everything else. Nor do I believe it can contain or resist the gathering forces of change without committing suicide in the process.

needs are easily satisfied and that the resources for doing so are plentiful. Competition is unnecessary and the only danger to humans is human aggression. There is no reason outside of human perversity for peace not to reign and for life not to be spent in the cultivation of joy and beauty. Those who can do this in the face of the old culture's ubiquity are considered "beautiful."

The flaw in the new culture is the fact that the old culture has succeeded in hiding the cornucopia of satisfactions that the new assumes—that a certain amount of work is required to release the bounty that exists from the restraints under which it is now placed. Whereas the flaw in the old culture has caused it to begin to decompose, the flaw in the new culture has produced a profound schism in its ranks—a schism between activist and dropout approaches to the culture as it now exists. We will return to this problem a little later.

It is important to recognize the internal logic of the old culture, however absurd its premise. If one assumes scarcity, then the knowledge that others want the same things that we have leads with some logic to preparations for defense, and, ultimately (since the best defense is offense), for attack. The same assumption leads to a high value being placed on the ability to postpone gratification (since there is not enough to go around). The expression of feelings is a luxury, since it might alert the scarce resources to the fact that the hunter is near.

The high value placed on restraint and coldness (which, as the Beatles observe in the epigraph for this chapter, creates even greater scarcity) generates in turn another norm: that of "good taste." One can best understand the meaning of such a norm by examining what is common to those acts considered to be in violation of it, and on this basis the meaning of "good taste" is very clear. "Good taste" means tasteless in the literal sense. Any act or product which contains too much stimulus value is considered to be "in bad taste" by old-culture adherents. Since gratification is viewed as a scarce commodity, arousal is dangerous. Clothes must be drab and inconspicuous, colors of low intensity, smells nonexistent ("if it weren't for bad taste there wouldn't be no taste at all"). Sounds should be quiet, words should lack affect. Four-letter words are always in bad taste because they have high stimulus value. Satire is in bad taste if it arouses political passions or creates images that are too vivid or exciting. All direct references to sexuality are in bad taste until proven innocent, since sexual arousal is the most feared result of all. The lines in old-culture homes, furnishings, and public buildings are hard and utilitarian. Since auditory overstimulation is more familiarly painful than its visual counterpart, brilliant, intense, vibrant colors are called "loud," and the preferred colors for old-culture homes are dull and listless. Stimulation in any form leaves old-culture Americans with a "bad taste" in their mouths. This taste is the taste of desire—a reminder that life in the here-and-now contains many pleasures to distract them from the carrot dangling beyond their reach. Too much stimulation makes the carrot hard to see. Good taste is a taste for carrots.

In the past decade, however, this pattern has undergone a merciless assault from the new culture. For if we assume that gratification is easy and resources plentiful, stimulation is no longer to be feared. Psychedelic colors, amplified sound, erotic books and films, bright and elaborate clothing, spicy food, "intense" (i.e., Anglo-Saxon) words, angry and irreverent satire—all go counter to the old pattern of understimulation. Long hair and beards provide a more "tactile" appearance than the bland, shaven-and-shorn, geometric lines of the fifties. Even Edward Hall's accusation that America is a land of "olfactory blandness" (a statement any traveler will confirm) must now be qualified a little, as the smells of coffee shops, foreign cooking, and incense combine to breathe a modicum of sensation even into the olfactory sphere. (Hall is right, however, in the sense that when America is filled with intense color, music, and ornament, deodorants will be the old culture's last-ditch holdouts. It is no accident that hostility to hippies so often focuses on their olfactory humanity.) The old culture turned the volume down on emotional experience in order to concentrate on its dreams of glory, but the new culture has turned it up again.

New-culture adherents, in fact, often display symptoms of *under*sensitivity to stimuli. They say "Wow!" in response to almost everything, but in voices utterly devoid of either tension or affect. They seem in general to be more certain that desire can be gratified than that it can be aroused.

This phenomenon probably owes much to early child-rearing

conditions. Under ordinary circumstances a mother responds to her child's needs when they are expressed powerfully enough to distract her from other cares and activities. Mothers who overrespond to the Spockian challenge, however, often try to anticipate the child's needs. Before arousal has proceeded very far they hover about and try several possible satisfactions. Since we tend to use these early parental responses as models for the way we treat our own impulses in adulthood, some new-culture adherents find themselves moving toward gratification before need arousal is clear or compelling. Like their mothers they are not altogether clear which need they are feeling. To make matters worse they are caught in the dilemma that spontaneity automatically evaporates the moment it becomes an ideology. It is a paradox of the modern condition that only those who oppose complete libidinal freedom are capable of ever achieving it.

Another logical consequence of scarcity assumptions is structured inequality. If there is not enough to go around then those who have more will find ways to prolong their advantage, and even legitimate it through various devices. The law itself, although philosophically committed to equality, is fundamentally a social device for maintaining structured systems of inequality (defining as crimes, for example, only those forms of theft and violence in which lower class persons engage). One of the major thrusts of the new culture, on the other hand, is equality: since the good things of life are plentiful, everyone should share them: rich and poor, black and white, female and male.

It is a central characteristic of the old culture that means habitually become ends, and ends means. Instead of people working in order to obtain goods in order to be happy, for example, we find that people should be made happy in order to work better in order to obtain more goods, and so on. Inequality, originally a consequence of scarcity, is now a means of creating artificial scarcities. For in the old culture, as we have seen, the manufacture of scarcity is the principal activity. Hostile comments of old-culture adherents toward new-culture forms ("people won't want to work if they can get things for nothing," "people won't want to get married if they can get it free") often reveal this preoccupation. Scarcity, the presumably undesired but unavoidable foundation for the whole old-culture edifice, has now become its most treasured and sacred value, and to maintain this value in the midst of plenty it has been necessary to establish invidiousness as the foremost criterion of worth. Old-culture Americans are peculiarly drawn to anything that seems to be the exclusive possession of some group or other, and find it difficult to enjoy anything they themselves have unless they can be sure that there are people to whom this pleasure is denied. For those in power even life itself derives its value invidiously: amid the emptiness and anesthesia of a power-oriented career many officials derive reassurance of their vitality from their proximity to the possibility of blowing up the world.

The centrality of invidiousness offers a strong barrier to the diffusion of social justice and equality. But it provides a *raison d'être* for the advertising industry, whose primary function is to manufacture illusions of scarcity. In a society engorged to the point of strangulation with useless and joyless products, advertisements show people calamitously running out of their food or beer, avidly hoarding potato chips, stealing each other's cigarettes, guiltily borrowing each other's deodorants, and so on. In a land of plenty there is little to fight over, but in the world of advertising images men and women will fight before changing their brand, in a kind of parody of the Vietnam war.

The fact that property takes precedence over human life in the old culture also follows logically from scarcity assumptions. If possessions are scarce relative to people they come to have more value than people. This is especially true of people with few possessions, who come to be considered so worthless as to be subhuman and hence eligible for extermination. Many possessions, on the other hand, entitle the owner to a status somewhat more than human. But as a society becomes more affluent these priorities begin to change—human life increases in value and property decreases. New-culture adherents challenge the high relative value placed on property, although the old priority still permeates the society's normative structure. It is still considered permissible, for example, to kill someone who is stealing your property under certain conditions. This is especially true if that person is without property himself—a wealthy kleptomaniac (in contrast to a poor black looter) would probably be worth a murder trial if killed while stealing.*

A recent sign of the shift in values was the *Pueblo* courtmartial. While the Navy, standing firmly behind old-culture priorities, argued that the Commander of the spy ship should have sacrificed the lives of ninety men to prevent the loss of "expensive equipment" to the enemy, the public at large supported his having put human life first. Much of the intense legal upheaval visible today—expressed most noticeably in the glare of publicity that now attaches to the activities of the U.S. Supreme Court—derives from the attempt to adapt an old-culture legal system to the changing priorities that render it obsolete.

It would not be difficult to show how the other characteristics of the old culture are based on the same scarcity assumptions, or to trace out in detail the derivation of the new culture from the premise that life's satisfactions exist in abundance and sufficiency for all. Let us instead look more closely at the relationship that the new culture bears to the old—the continuities and discontinuities that it offers—and explore some of the contradictions it holds within itself.

First of all it should be stressed that affluence and economic security are not in themselves responsible for the new culture. The rich, like the poor, have always been with us to some degree, but the new culture has not. What is significant in the new culture is not a celebration of economic affluence but a rejection of its foundation. The new culture is concerned with rejecting the artificial scarcities upon which material abundance is based. It argues that instead of throwing away one's body so that one can accumulate material artifacts, one should throw away the artifacts and enjoy one's body. The new culture is not merely blindly reactive, however, but embodies a sociological consciousness. In this consciousness lies the key insight that possessions actually generate scarcity. The more emotion one invests in them the more chances for significant gratification are lost—the more committed to them one be-

---

* A more trivial example can be found in the old culture's handling of noise control. Police are called to prevent distraction by the joyous noises of laughter and song, but not to stop the harsh and abrasive roar of power saws, air hammers, power mowers, snow blowers, and other baneful machines.

comes the more deprived one feels, like a thirsty man drinking salt water. To accumulate possessions is to deliver pieces of oneself to dead things. Possessions can absorb an emotional cathexis, but unlike personal relationships they feed nothing back. Americans have combined the proliferation of possessions with the disruption, circumscription, and trivialization of most personal relationships. An alcoholic becomes malnourished because drinking obliterates his hunger. Americans become unhappy and vicious because their preoccupation with amassing possessions obliterates their loneliness. This is why production in America seems to be on such an endless upward spiral: every time we buy something we deepen our emotional deprivation and hence our need to buy something. This is good for business, of course, but those who profit most from this process are just as trapped in the general deprivation as everyone else. The new-culture adherents are thus not merely affluent—they are trying to substitute an adequate emotional diet for a crippling addiction.

The new culture is nevertheless a product of the old, not merely a rejection of it. It picks up themes latent or dormant or subordinate in the old and magnifies them. The hippie movement, for example, is brimming with nostalgia—a nostalgia peculiarly American and shared by old-culture adherents. This nostalgia embraces the Old West, Amerindian culture, the wilderness, the simple life, the utopian community—all venerable American traditions. But for the old culture they represent a subordinate, ancillary aspect of the culture, appropriate for recreational occasions or fantasy representation—a kind of pastoral relief from everyday striving—whereas for the new culture they are dominant themes. The new culture's passion for memorabilia, paradoxically, causes uneasiness in old-culture adherents, whose future-oriented invidiousness leads to a desire to sever themselves from the past. Yet for the most part it is a question of the new culture making the old culture's secondary themes primary, rather than simply seeking to discard the old culture's primary theme. Even the notion of "dropping out" is an important American tradition—neither the United States itself nor its populous suburbs would exist were this not so.

Americans have always been deeply ambivalent about the issue of social involvement. On the one hand they are suspicious of it and share deep romantic fantasies of withdrawal to a simple pastoral or even sylvan life. On the other hand they are much given to acting out grandiose fantasies of taking society by storm, through the achievement of wealth, power, or fame. This ambivalence has led to many strange institutions—the suburb and the automobile being the most obvious. But note that both fantasies express the viewpoint of an outsider. Americans have a profound tendency to feel like outsiders—they wonder where the action is and wander about in search of it (this puts an enormous burden on celebrities, who are supposed to know, but in fact feel just as doubtful as everyone else). Americans have created a society in which they are automatically nobodies, since no one has any stable place or enduring connection. The village idiot of earlier times was less a "nobody" in this sense than the mobile junior executive or academic. An American has to "make a place for himself" because he does not have one.

Since the society rests on scarcity assumptions, involvement in it has always meant competitive involvement, and, curiously enough, the theme of bucolic withdrawal has often associated itself with that of cooperative, communal life. So consistently, in fact, have intentional communities established themselves in the wilderness that one can only infer that society as we know it makes cooperative life impossible.

Be that as it may, it is important to remember that the New England colonies grew out of utopian communes, so that the dropout tradition is not only old but extremely important to our history. Like so many of the more successful nineteenth century utopian communities (Oneida and Amana, for example) the puritans became corrupted by involvement in successful economic enterprise and the communal aspect was eroded away—another example of a system being destroyed by what it attempts to ignore. The new culture is thus a kind of reform movement, attempting to revive a decayed tradition once important to our civilization.

In stressing these continuities between the new culture and the American past, I do not mean to imply a process unique to our society. One of the most basic characteristics of all successful social systems—indeed, perhaps all living matter as well—is that they include devices that serve to keep alive alternatives that are antithetical to their dominant emphases, as a kind of hedge against change. These latent alternatives usually persist in some encapsulated and imprisoned form ("break glass in case of fire"), such as myths, festivals, or specialized roles. Fanatics continually try to expunge these circumscribed contradictions, but when they succeed it is often fatal to the society. For, as Lewis Mumford once pointed out, it is the "laxity, corruption, and disorder" in a system that makes it viable, considering the contradictory needs that all social systems must satisfy.[2] Such latent alternatives are priceless treasures and must be carefully guarded against loss. For a new cultural pattern does not emerge out of nothing—the seed must already be there, like the magic tricks of wizards and witches in folklore, who can make an ocean out of a drop of water, a palace out of a stone, a forest out of a blade of grass, but nothing out of nothing. Many peoples keep alive a tradition of a golden age, in which a totally different social structure existed. The Judeo-Christian God, patriarchal and omnipotent, has served in matrifocal cultures to keep alive the concept of a strong and protective paternal figure in the absence of real-life examples. Jesters kept alive a wide variety of behavior patterns amid the stilted and restrictive formality of royal courts. The specialized effeminate roles that one finds in many warrior cultures are not merely a refuge for those who fail to succeed in the dominant pattern—they are also a living reminder that the rigid "protest masculinity" that prevails is not the only conceivable kind of behavior for a male. And conversely, the warrior ethos is maintained in a peaceful society or era by means of a military cadre or reserve system.

These phenomena are equivalent to (and in literate cultures tend increasingly to be replaced by) written records of social practices. They are like a box of seldom-used tools, or a trunk of old costumes awaiting the proper period-play. Suddenly the environment changes, the tolerated eccentric becomes a prophet, the clown a dancing-master, the doll an idol, the idol a doll. The elements have not changed, only the arrangement and the emphases have changed. Every revolution is in part a revival.

Sometimes societal ambivalence is so marked that the latent pattern is retained in a form almost as elaborated as the dominant one. Our society, for example, is one of the most mobile (geographically, at least) ever known; yet, unlike other nomadic cultures it makes little allowance for this fact in its patterns of material accumulation. Our homes are furnished as if we intended to spend the rest of our lives in them, instead of moving every few years. This perhaps represents merely a kind of technological neurosis—a yearning for stability expressed in a technological failure to adapt. Should Americans ever settle down, however, they will find little to do in the way of readjusting their household furnishing habits.

Ultimately it seems inevitable that Americans must either abandon their nomadic habits (which seems unlikely) or moderate their tendency to invest their libido exclusively in material possessions (an addiction upon which the economy relies rather heavily). The new culture is of course pushing hard to realize the second alternative, and if it is successful one might anticipate a trend toward more simply furnished dwellings in which all but the most portable and decorative items are permanent installations. In such a case we might like or dislike a sofa or bed or dresser, but would have no more personal involvement with it than we now do with a stove, furnace, or garage. We would possess, cathect, feel as a part of us, only a few truly personal and portable items.

This tendency of human societies to keep alternative patterns alive has many biological analogues. One of these is *neoteny*—the evolutionary process in which foetal or juvenile characteristics are retained in the adult animal. Body characteristics that have long had only transitional relevance are exploited in response to altered environmental circumstances (thus many human features resemble foetal traits of apes). I have not chosen this example at random, for much of the new culture is implicitly and explicitly "neotenous" in a cultural sense: behavior, values, and life-styles formerly seen as appropriate only to childhood are being retained into adulthood as a counterforce to the old culture.

I pointed out earlier, for example, that children are taught a set of values in earliest childhood—cooperation, sharing, equalitarianism —which they begin to unlearn as they enter school, wherein competition, invidiousness, status differentiation, and ethnocentrism prevail. By the time they enter adult life children are expected to have largely abandoned the value assumptions with which their social lives began. But for affluent, protected, middle-class children this process is slowed down, while intellectual development is speeded up, so that the earlier childhood values can become integrated into a conscious, adult value system centered around social justice. The same is true of other characteristics of childhood: spontaneity, hedonism, candor, playfulness, use of the senses for pleasure rather than utility, and so on. The protective, child-oriented, middle-class family allows the child to preserve some of these qualities longer than is possible under more austere conditions, and his intellectual precocity makes it possible for him to integrate them into an ideological system with which he can confront the corrosive, life-abusing tendencies of the old culture.

When these neotenous characteristics become manifest to old-culture adherents the effect is painfully disturbing, for they vibrate feelings and attitudes that are very old and very deep, although long and harshly stifled. Old-culture adherents have learned to reject all this, but since the learning antedated intellectual maturity they have no coherent ideological framework within which such a rejection can be consciously understood and thoughtfully endorsed. They are deeply attracted and acutely revolted at the same time. They can neither resist their fascination nor control their antipathy. This is exemplified by the extravagant curiosity that hippie communes attract, and by the harassment that so often extinguishes them.[3] It is usually necessary in such situations for the rote-learned abhorrence to discharge itself in persecutory activity before the more positive responses can be released. This was true in the case of the early Christians in Rome, with whom contemporary hippies are often compared (both were communal, utopian, mystical, dropouts, unwashed; both were viewed as dangerous, masochistic, ostentatious, the cause of their own troubles; both existed in societies in which the exclusive pursuit of material advantages had reached some kind of dead end), and seems equally true today. The absorption of this persecution is part of the process through which the latent values that the oppressed group protects and nurtures are expropriated by the majority and released into the mainstream of the culture.

Up to this point we have (rather awkwardly) discussed the new culture as if it were an integrated, monolithic pattern, which is certainly very far from the case. There are many varied and contradictory streams feeding the new culture, and some of these deserve particular attention, since they provide the raw material for future axes of conflict.

The most glaring split in the new culture is that which separates militant activism from the traits we generally associate with the hippie movement. The first strand stresses political confrontation, revolutionary action, radical commitment to the process of changing the basic structure of modern industrial society. The second involves a renunciation of that society in favor of the cultivation of inner experience and pleasing internal feeling-states. Heightening of sensory receptivity, commitment to the immediate present, and tranquil acceptance of the physical environment are sought in contradistinction to old-culture ways, in which the larger part of one's immediate experience is overlooked or grayed out by the preoccupation with utility, future goals, and external mastery. Since, in the old culture, experience is classified before it is felt, conceptualization tends here to be forsworn altogether. There is also much emphasis on aesthetic expression and an overarching belief in the power of love.

This division is a crude one, and there are, of course, many areas of overlap. Both value systems share an antipathy to the old culture, both share beliefs in sexual freedom and personal autonomy. Some groups (the Yippies, in particular) have tried with some success to bridge the gap in a variety of interesting ways. But there is nonetheless an inherent contradiction between them. Militant activism is task-oriented, and hence partakes of certain old-culture traits such as postponement of gratification, preoccupation with power, and so on. To be a competent revolutionary one must possess a certain tolerance for the "Protestant Ethic" virtues, and the activists' moral code is a stern one indeed. The hippie ethic, on the other hand, is a "salvation now" approach. It is thus more radical, since it remains relatively uncontaminated with old-culture values. It is also far less realistic, since it ignores the fact that the existing culture provides a totally antagonistic milieu in which the hippie movement must try to survive in a state of highly vulnerable parasitic dependence. The activists can reasonably say that the flower people are absurd to pretend that the revolution has already occurred, for such pretense leads only to severe victimization by the old culture. The flower people can reasonably retort that a revolution based to so great a degree on old-culture premises is lost before it is begun, for even if the militants are victorious they will have been corrupted by the process of winning.

The dilemma is a very real one and arises whenever radical change is sought. For every social system attempts to exercise the most rigid control over the mechanisms by which it can be altered —defining some as legitimate and others as criminal or disloyal. When we examine the characteristics of legitimate and nonlegitimate techniques, however, we find that the "legitimate" ones involve a course of action requiring a sustained commitment to the core assumptions of the culture. In other words, if the individual follows the "legitimate" pathway there is a very good chance that his initial radical intent will be eroded in the process. If he feels that some fundamental change in the system is required, then, he has a choice between following a path that subverts his goal or one that leads him to be jailed as a criminal or traitor.

This process is not a Machiavellian invention of American capitalists, but rather a mechanism which all viable social systems must evolve spontaneously in order to protect themselves from instability. When the system as it stands is no longer viable, however, the mechanism must be exposed for the swindle that it is; otherwise the needed radical changes will be rendered ineffectual.

The key to the mechanism is the powerful human reluctance to admit that an achieved goal was not worth the unpleasant experience required to achieve it.[4] This is the basic principle underlying initiation rituals: "if I had to suffer so much pain and humiliation to get into this club it must be a wonderful organization." The evidence of thousands of years is that the mechanism works extremely well. Up to some point, for example, war leaders can count on high casualties to increase popular commitment to military adventures.

Thus when a political leader says to a militant, "why don't you run for political office (get a haircut, dress conservatively, make deals, do the dirty work for your elders) and try to change the system in that way"—or the teacher says to the student, "wait until you have your Ph.D. (M.D., LL.B.) and then you can criticize our program," or the white man says to the black man, "when you begin to act like us you'll receive the same opportunities we do"—there is a serious subterfuge involved (however unconscious it may be) in that the protester, if he accepts the condition, will in most cases be automatically converted by it to his opponent's point of view.

The dilemma of the radical, then, is that he is likely to be corrupted if he fights the *status quo* on its own terms, but is not permitted to fight it in any other way. The real significance of the New Left is that it has discovered, in the politics of confrontation, as near a solution to this dilemma as can be found: it is always a bit problematic whether the acts of the new militants are "within the system" or not, and substantial headway can be made in the resulting confusion.

Yet even here the problem remains: if an activist devotes his life to altering the power structure, will he not become like old-culture adherents—utilitarian, invidious, scarcity-oriented, future-centered, and so on? Having made the world safe for flower people will he be likely to relinquish it to them? "You tell me it's the institution," object the Beatles, "you'd better free your mind instead." But what if all the freed minds are in jail?

The dilemma is particularly clear for blacks. Some blacks are much absorbed in rediscovering and celebrating those characteristics which seem most distinctively black and in sharpest contrast to white Western culture: black expressiveness, creativity, sensuality, and spontaneity being opposed to white constrictedness, rigidity, frigidity, bustle, and hypocrisy. For these blacks, to make too great a commitment to the power game is to forsake one's blackness. Power is a white hangup. Yet the absence of power places rather severe limits on the ability of blacks to realize their blackness or anything else.

There is no way to resolve this dilemma, and indeed, it is probably better left unresolved. In a revolutionary situation one needs discipline and unity of purpose, which, however, leads to all kinds of abuses when the goal is won. Discipline and unity become ends in themselves (after the old-culture pattern) and the victory becomes an empty one. It is therefore of great importance to have the envisioned revolutionary goals embodied in a group culture of some kind, with which the acts of those in power can be compared. In the meantime the old culture is subject to a two-pronged attack: a direct assault from activists—unmasking its life-destroying proclivities, its corruption, its futility and pointlessness, its failure to achieve any of its objectives—and an indirect assault by the expansion of expressive countercultures beyond a tolerable (i.e., freak) size.

Closely related to the activist-hippie division is the conflict over the proper role of aggression in the new culture. Violence is a major theme in the old culture and most new-culture adherents view human aggression with deep suspicion. Nonviolence has been the dominant trend in both the activist and hippie segments of the new culture until recently. But more and more activists have become impatient with the capacity of the old culture to strike the second cheek with even more enthusiasm than the first, and have endorsed violence under certain conditions as a necessary evil.

For the activists the issue has been practical rather than ideological: most serious and thoughtful activists have only a tactical commitment to violence. For the dropout ideologues, however, aggression poses a difficult problem: if they seek to minimize the artificial constriction of emotional expression, how can they be consistently loving and pacific? This logical dilemma is usually resolved by ignoring it: the love cult typically represses aggressive feelings ruthlessly—the body is paramount only so long as it is a loving body.

At the moment the old culture is so fanatically absorbed in violence that it does the work for everyone. If the new culture should prevail, however, the problem of human aggression would probably be its principal bone of contention. Faced with the persistence of aggressiveness (even in the absence of the old culture's exaggerated violence-inducing institutions), the love cult will be forced to re-examine its premises, and opt for some combination of expression and restraint that will restore human aggression to its rightful place as a natural, though secondary, human emotion.

A third split in the new culture is the conflict between individualism and collectivism. On this question the new culture talks out of both sides of its mouth, one moment pitting ideals of cooperation and community against old-culture competitiveness, the next moment espousing the old culture in its most extreme form with exhortations to "do your own thing." I am not arguing that individualism need be totally extirpated in order to make community possible, but new-culture enterprises often collapse because of a dogmatic unwillingness to subordinate the whim of the individual to the needs of the group. This problem is rarely faced honestly by new-culture adherents, who seem unaware of the conservatism involved in their attachment to individualistic principles.

It is always disastrous to attempt to eliminate any structural principle altogether; but if the balance between individualistic and collective emphases in America is not altered, everything in the new culture will be perverted and caricatured into simply another bizarre old-culture product. There must be continuities between the old and the new, but these cannot extend to the relative weights assigned to core motivational principles. The new culture seeks to create a tolerable society within the context of persistent American strivings—utopianism, the pursuit of happiness. But nothing will change until individualism is assigned a subordinate place in the American value system—for individualism lies at the core of the old culture, and a prepotent individualism is not a viable foundation for any society in a nuclear age.

6

The postponed life

To live through a revolution is a delirious experience.
SEALE AND MC CONVILLE

*I promise you that in the joy and laughter of the festival
nobody will . . . dare to put a sinister interpretation on
your sudden return to human shape.*
APULEIUS

*Please don't be long
For I may be asleep.*
HARRISON

Sociology does not contain a special subfield, like clinical psychology, devoted to the diagnosis and treatment of societal malfunction.
Social workers may treat and classify the human *victims* of such
malfunction, but rarely the malfunctions themselves. When sociologists are involved in such activities the enterprise is altogether
different from that of the clinical psychologist or psychiatrist, who
can engage in a direct, prolonged, and authoritative confrontation
with the object of his ministrations under relatively controlled conditions. A sociologist is engaged by persons rather than a system,
and his access to that system is generally rather sharply curtailed
by his clients, who, their lives having been devoted to the acquisition of power, are understandably reluctant to relinquish its exercise
to persons not having made a comparable sacrifice.

What, then, can a book of this kind say when it comes to utiliz-
ing whatever insight has been gained through analysis? Talk is
cheap, and perhaps the wisest course for a social analyst at such a

moment is to be quiet, and let those who are gifted at social action make whatever use of the analysis they can. Still, to suggest that a society is in a disastrous state without offering any guides to action implies a detachment so extreme as to disqualify the analysis.

Fortunately, there is no need to discuss ways of initiating change, since change is already in motion. At the same time, however, the pathology of the old culture is accelerating, so that the dangers it produces grow concomitantly with the possibility of rescue. The two cultures race in opposite directions, pulling the society apart: our task is to optimize the transition from one pattern of cultural dominance to the other. To do this we must first explore some of the ambiguities and paradoxes of social change.

REVOLUTION AND CHANGE

Revolutionaries look with justifiable contempt upon gradualism, which generally proves not to be change at all, but merely an exercise in conservative ingenuity. Furthermore, there is no place for gradualism in a life-or-death situation—one does not walk sedately out of the way when about to be run over by a truck. This is the crux of all arguments between old- and new-culture adherents: if there is no crisis then the impatience and aggressiveness of activists is inappropriate. But if there *is* a crisis, then the militants are showing great restraint as it is. To my mind the crisis is self-evident, and the blandness exhibited by old-culture adherents in the face of it is difficult to explain without recourse to psychopathology.

C. Wright Mills coined the term "crackpot realism" to characterize the kind of short-run, parochial thinking that finds itself unable to reconsider an existing policy, no matter how disastrous. A crackpot realist is an administrator who throws away a million dollars because "you can't just junk a project we've put a hundred thousand dollars into." Crackpot realists cite "practical politics" to defend our support of tottering dictatorial regimes that have collapsed one after the other (indeed, our policy of trying to outbid the Soviet Union for white elephants has made our greatest defeats look, in retrospect, like clever stratagems).

Crackpot realism also renders us incapable of guarding ourselves against the mortal domestic hazards we create. Although the devastation wrought by DDT, for example, has been firmly established for years, lawmakers even now talk of a "timetable" for phasing it out. (If we discovered arsenic in our flour bin would we construct a "timetable" for phasing out the flour?) And when a miscalculation at Dugway caused nerve gas to drift halfway to Salt Lake City, killing 6000 sheep en route, government officials did not reassess the desirability of manufacturing such poisons and spraying them into our atmosphere.* Finally, crackpot realism argues that we must move slowly in handling urban problems, despite the fact that ghetto conditions annually manufacture thousands of stunted minds, burnt-out cases, and killers. The middle-class "realist's" neglect nurtures today the disturbed freak who will kill his child tomorrow. But it is not "practical" in America to make drastic changes, even to save lives.

Yet there is a sense in which all change is gradual. There is an illusory element in revolutionary change—a tendency to exaggerate the efficacy of the revolutionary moment by ignoring the subtle and undramatic changes leading up to that moment, and the reactions, corruptions, and compromises that follow it. The revolutionary moment is like a "breakthrough" in scientific discovery, or in psychotherapy. It is dramatic and exciting and helps motivate the dreary process of retooling society (or scientific thought, or the personality structure) piece by tedious piece. It may be necessary for any real change to occur at all—even the kinds of changes that liberal reformers seek. The only reason for stressing the latent gradualism in revolution is that revolutionaries typically expend much of their energy attacking those very groups that undertake the "softening-up" work that makes revolution possible.

Such internecine warfare often revolves around the notion that

---

* Another feature of crackpot realism is the policy of automatic lying adopted by public officials and corporation executives when caught with their fingers in the cookie jar. The Pentagon and the State Department are the most incorrigible in this respect, but the automobile executives who tried to "get something on" Ralph Nader showed a cinematic knowledgeability that appealed to aficionados of old Bogart films. On the whole, however, the when-in-doubt-lie-for-a-while approach has been an important source of youthful hostility to old-culture leaders.

correct radical strategy seeks to "make things worse" in order to encourage a revolutionary confrontation between the forces of reaction and the revolutionary saviors. In this view any liberal efforts at social amelioration are to be avoided as dampers on revolutionary fervor. One attempts instead to bring about a situation so repressive and disagreeable that the masses will be forced to call on the revolutionaries, waiting in the wings. (This kind of fatuous policy helped bring to power Hitler, who saw to it that the revolutionaries did their waiting in concentration camps.) But provoking repression is an effective technique only if the repression itself is confused and anarchic. The result of "things getting bad enough" is usually to demoralize most of those who want change and to intimidate a good many more. Revolution does not occur when things get bad enough but when things get better—when small improvements generate rising aspirations and decrease tolerance for long-existing injustices. The "make things worse" approach is not only not strategic, it is not even revolutionary—it seeks unconsciously to preserve, while at the same time discrediting, parental authority. The emotional logic behind it might be expressed as: "if things get bad enough They will see that it is unfair." As every radical knows, radical movements are always plagued with people who want to lose, want to be stopped, want in effect to be put under protective custody.

This is not an argument for moderation—taking an extreme position can be a winning as well as a losing stance. But when changes in the desired direction are opposed *because* they keep things from getting bad enough, we can assume at the very least that the attitude toward change is highly ambivalent.

The make-it-worse position is based on the same assumption as the "backlash" position, which argues that "if you go too far They will turn against you." Both view public opinion as a kind of judicial Good Parent, and exaggerate the importance of transient public sentiment. Both underestimate the importance, for creating change, of prolonged exposure to new ideas. There is no such thing as a situation so intolerable that human beings must necessarily rise up against it. People can bear anything, and the longer it exists the more placidly they will bear it. The job of the revolutionary is to show people that things *can* be better and to move them directly and unceasingly toward that goal. The better things get the more aware people become that they need not tolerate the injustices and miseries that remain. By the same token, the worst backlash situation is always better than the pre-change condition. Backlash implies that people once accepted and then came to reject change, but this is not the case. It is merely that the significance of the change—the reality of it—was not yet understood. Backlash is simply part of the educative process—the process of learning that change means change.

It is behavior and institutions that the true revolutionary seeks to change—the good or bad opinion of those around him is of little consequence. The backlash-avoider is saying, "if we go too far people will think badly of me." This is true, but irrelevant. The distinction is often made: "Yes, change is necessary, but some of the leaders (militants, radicals) go too far." This distinction is useful for it allows the conservative to discharge his anxiety, discomfort, and resentment onto individuals while learning gradually to accept the changes those individuals are creating. Similarly, the make-things-worse advocate is saying, "if things get bad enough even I will look good by comparison and people will think well of me and say that I am right." Better that he be thought a silly eccentric and progress be made.

Change can take place only when liberal and radical pressures are both strong. Intelligent liberals have always recognized the debt they owe to radicals, whose existence permits liberals to push further than they would otherwise have dared, all the while posing as compromisers and mediators. Radicals, however, have been somewhat less sensible of their debt to liberals, partly because of the rather single-minded discipline radicals are almost forced to maintain, plagued as they always are by liberal backsliding and timidity on the one hand and various forms of self-destructiveness and romantic posing on the other.

Yet liberal adjustments often do much to soften up an initially rigid *status quo*—creating just those rising expectations that make revolutionary change possible. Radicals often object that liberal programs generate an illusory feeling of movement when in fact little is changing. Their assumption is always that such an illusion slows down movement, but it is just as likely that the reverse is true. Radicals are so absorbed with the difficulties they have in overcoming inertia that they tend to assume that motionlessness is a comfortable state that everyone will seek with the slightest excuse. But even an illusory sense of progress is invigorating, and whets the desire for further advances. Absolute stagnation is enervating, and creates a feeling of helplessness and impotence. The "war on poverty" may have done very little to alleviate poverty and nothing at all to remove its causes, but it raised a lot of expectations, created many visions of the possibilities for change, alerted a large number of people to existing inadequacies in the system and to the relative efficacy of various strategies for eliminating them. One factor that radicals overlook, in other words, is the educative value of liberal reform, however insignificant that reform may be in terms of institutional change.

Liberal reform and radical change are thus complementary rather than antagonistic. Together they make it possible continually to test the limits of what can be done. Liberals never know whether the door is unlocked because they are afraid to try it. Radicals, on the other hand, miss many opportunities for small advances because they are unwilling to settle for so little. No one group can possibly fulfill both these functions—constant testing of the maximum prohibits constant testing of the minimum and vice versa.

The activist-hippie split within the radical group is a similar but more serious division. One group seeks to redirect the old striving pattern to social goals—to build a revolutionary new society instead of empires and fortunes—while the other seeks to abolish the old striving pattern itself. One seeks to remake the world to make it tolerable for us to live in, the other tries to cure us of our need to remake the world.

The conflict expresses itself ideologically in the argument as to whether one should attempt to change institutions or the motivational patterns associated with those institutions. Positions on this question tend to be based on whether one thinks the motivational patterns created the institutions or vice versa. Now the first task of a system is to maintain itself, and every system must therefore contain mechanisms to reactivate continually the motivational eccentricities that gave rise to it in the first place. Still, one cannot avoid a feeling of skepticism when it is proposed that institutional change alone will bring about motivational change. Closing down gambling casinos may reduce the volume of gambling but it does not end it. Institutions, like technology, are materializations of the fantasies of a past generation, inflicted on the present. Unless there is reason to believe these fantasies have changed there is little point in trying to change the institutions, since they will simply reemerge. On the other hand, one can no longer approach the problem psychologically once the fantasies have achieved institutional form, since they now represent reality—a reality in which subsequent fantasies will be rooted.

Motivation and institutional structure are thus twinned, like the hedgehog and his wife in the folktale, and those who would bring about change are like the frantic hare, who, racing to best the one, finds he has been outdistanced by the other. Change can take place only when institutions have been analyzed, discredited, and disassembled, and the motivational forces that gave rise to them redirected into alternative spheres of gratification. Change without either of these two contradictory approaches will be short-lived or illusory.

The revolutionary must learn to live with such contradictions. Intellectuals are much too fond of playing out a romantic fantasy in which they, as lonely heroes, battle bravely against a crass multitude and/or a totalitarian social structure. We are no more likely than anyone else to recognize the ways in which our own behavior generates the forces that plague us from outside; as in the case of all private myths the hero is merely an injured innocent.

But the impersonal, intricate, omnivorous machinery that threatens, benumbs, and bureaucratizes the helpless individual in Marcuse's *One-Dimensional Man* is not something external to the individual; it *is* the individual—the grotesque materialization of his turning away. Marcuse quotes with approval a passage from René Dubos stressing the importance of "the longing for quiet, privacy, independence, initiative, and some open space," and suggests that capitalism not only prevents it from being gratified but also numbs the longing itself.[1] It is not clear on what basis he decides that the longing for privacy is numbed in our society—one would be hard put to find a society anywhere in which the search was more desperate, or generated a greater wealth of cultural inventions (largely self-defeating). The longing for quiet, privacy, independence, initiative, and open space is the foundation-stone of American society —of the suburb, the highway, and the entire technological monstrosity which threatens to engulf us. The longing itself is not a fundamental or driving human motive, but a reaction to crowding, complexity, and social dislocation. Those who live in stable preindustrial communities have far less privacy and far less desire for it than we do. They feel less manipulated and intruded upon only because they can predict and influence their daily social encounters with greater ease. The longing for privacy is generated by the drastic conditions that the longing for privacy produces.

STRANGERS IN PARADISE

We need now to consider seriously what the role of those over thirty is to be during the transition to and emergence of the new culture. Many will of course simply oppose it, with varying degrees of violence. A few will greet it with a sense of liberation, finding in it an answer they have long sought, but will experience a sense of awkwardness in trying to relate themselves to what has been so noisily appropriated by the young. Many more will be tormented with ambivalence, repelled by the new culture but disillusioned by the old.

It is to this latter group that what follows is addressed, for I do not believe that a successful transition can be made without their participation. If the issue is left to generational confrontation, with new-culture adherents attempting simply to push their elders out of the way and into the grave, the results will probably be catastrophic. The old culture will not simply fall of its own weight. It is not rotten but wildly malfunctioning, not weak and failing but strong and demented, not a sick old horse but a healthy runaway. It no longer performs its fundamental task of satisfying the needs of its adherents, but it still performs the task of feeding and perpetuating itself. Nor do the young have the knowledge and skill successfully to dismantle it. If the matter is left to the collision of generational change it seems to me inevitable that a radical-right revolution will occur as a last-ditch effort to stave off change.

Only those who have participated fully in the old culture can prevent this. Only they can dismantle the old culture without calamity. Furthermore, no revolution produces total change—much of the old machinery is retained more or less intact. Those intimate with the machinery are in the best position to facilitate the retooling and redirection.

But why should they? Why should they tear down what they have built? What place is there for them in the new culture? The new culture is contemptuous of age and rejects most of the values by which moderates have ordered their lives. Yet it must be remembered that the contempt for age and tradition, the worship of modernity, is not intrinsically a new-culture trait but a foundation-stone of a technology-dominated culture. It is the old culture that systematically invalidates learning and experience, that worships innovation and turns its back on the past, on familial and community ties. The new culture is preoccupied with tradition, with community, with relationships—with many things that would reinstate the validity of accumulated wisdom. Social change is replete with paradox, and one of the most striking is the fact that the old culture worships novelty, while the new would resuscitate a more tradition-oriented way of life. The rhetoric of short-run goals, in which the young shout down the present and shout up the future, masks the fact that in the long run there is more room for the aged in the new culture than in the old. This is something about which new-culture adherents, however, are also confused, and old-culture participants will have much to do to stake out a rightful place for age in the new culture. If they fail the new culture will be corrupted into a reactionary parody of itself.

My main argument for rejecting the old culture is that it has been unable to keep any of the promises that have sustained it for so long, and as it struggles more and more violently to maintain itself, it is less and less able to hide its fundamental antipathy to human life and human satisfaction. It spends hundreds of billions of dollars to find ways of killing more efficiently, but almost nothing to enhance the joys of living. Against those who sought to humanize their physical environment in Berkeley the forces of "law and order" used a poison gas outlawed by the Geneva Conventions. The old culture is unable to stop killing people—deliberately in the case of those who oppose it, with bureaucratic indifference in the case of those who obey its dictates or consume its products trustingly.

However familiar and comfortable it may seem, the old culture is threatening to kill us, like a trusted relative gone berserk so gradually that we are able to pretend to ourselves he has not changed.

But what can we cling to—what stability is there in our chaotic environment if we abandon the premises on which the old culture is based? To this I would answer that it is precisely these premises that have generated our chaotic environment. I recognize the desperate longing in America for stability, for some fixed reference point when all else is swirling about in endless flux. But to cling to old-culture premises is the act of a hopeless addict, who, when his increasingly expensive habit has destroyed everything else in his life, embraces his destroyer more fervently than ever. The radical change I am suggesting here is only the reinstatement of stability itself. It may appear highly unappealing, like all cold-turkey cures, but nothing else will stop the spiraling disruption to which our old-culture premises have brought us.

I am arguing, in other words, for a reversal of our old pattern of technological radicalism and social conservatism. Like most old-culture premises this is built upon a self-deception: we pretend that through it we actually achieve social stability—that technological change can be confined within its own sphere. Yet obviously this is not so. Technological instability creates social instability as well, and we lose both ways. Radical social change *has* occurred within the old culture, but unplanned and unheralded. The changes advocated by the new culture are changes that at least some people desire. The changes that have occurred under the old culture were desired by no one. They were not even foreseen. They just happened, and people tried to build a social structure around them; but it has always been a little like building sand castles in heavy surf and we have become a dangerously irritable people in the attempt. We have given technology carte blanche, much in the way Congress has always, in the past, given automatic approval to defense budgets, resulting in the most gigantic graft in history.

How long is it since anyone has said: "this is a pernicious invention, which will bring more misery than happiness to mankind?" Such comments occur only in horror and science-fiction films, and even there, in the face of the most calamitous outcomes that jaded and overtaxed brains can devise, the audience often feels a twinge of discomfort over the burning laboratory or the lost secret. Yet who would dare to defend even a small fraction of the technological innovations of the past century in terms of human satisfaction? The problem is that technology, industrialism, and capitalism have always been evaluated in their own terms. But it is absurd to evaluate capitalism in terms of the wealth it produces, or technology in terms of the inventions it generates, just as it would be absurd for a subway system to evaluate its service in terms of the number of tokens it manufactured. We need to find ways of appraising these systems in terms of criteria that are truly independent of the systems themselves. We need to develop a human-value index—a criterion that assesses the ultimate worth of an invention or a system or a product in terms of its total impact on human life, in terms of ends rather than means. We would then evaluate the achievements of medicine not in terms of man-hours of prolonged (and often comatose) life, or the volume of drugs sold, but in terms of the overall increase (or decrease) in human beings feeling healthy. We would evaluate city planning and .housing programs not in terms of the number of bodies incarcerated in a given location, or the number of millions given to contractors, but in terms of the extent to which people take joy in their surroundings. We would evaluate the worth of an industrial firm not in terms of the money made or the number of widgets manufactured or sold, or how distended the organization has become, but in terms of how much pleasure or satisfaction has been given to people. It is not without significance that we tend to appraise a nation today in terms of its gross national product—a phrase whose connotations speak for themselves.

The problem is particularly acute in the case of technology. Freud suggested forty years ago that the much-touted benefits of technology were "cheap pleasures," equivalent to the enjoyment obtained by "sticking one's bare leg outside the bedclothes on a cold winter's night and then drawing it in again." "If there were no railway to make light of distances," he pointed out, "my child would never have left home and I should not need the telephone to hear his voice."[2] Each technological "advance" is heralded as one that will solve problems created by its predecessors. None of them have done so, however, but have merely created new ones. Heroin was first introduced into this country as a heaven-sent cure for morphine

addicts, and this is the model followed by technological "progress."
We have been continually misled into supporting a larger and larger
technological habit.

Lest I be accused of exaggeration, let me quote from a recent
newspaper article: "How would you like to have your very own
flying saucer? One that you could park in the garage, take off and
land in your own driveway or office parking lot. . . . Within the
next few years you may own and fly just such an unusual aircraft
and consider it as common as driving the family automobile. . . ."
The writer goes on to describe a newly invented vertical-takeoff
aircraft which will cost no more to own and operate than a sports
car and is just as easy to drive. After an enthusiastic description of
the design of the craft he attributes its development to the inventor's "concern for the fate of the motorist," citing the inability of
the highways and city streets to handle the increasing number of
automobiles. The inventor claims that his saucer "will help solve
some of the big city traffic problems"![3]

The inventor is so confident of the public's groveling submission
to every technological command that he does not even bother to
defend this outlandish statement. Indeed, it is clear that he does not
believe it himself, since he brazenly predicts that every family in the
future will own a car *and* a saucer. He even acknowledges rather
flippantly that air traffic might become a difficulty, but suggests that
"these are not his problems," since he is "only the inventor."* He
goes on to note that his invention would be useful in military opera-
tions (such as machine-gunning oriental farmers and gassing stu-

* One is reminded of Tom Lehrer's brilliant song about the rocket
scientist:

"*Once they are up who cares where they come down:
That's not my department," says Werner Von Braun.*

The Nuremberg and Eichmann trials were attempts to reverse the general
rule that those who kill or make wretched a single person are severely punished, while those (heads of state, inventors, weapons manufacturers) who
are responsible for the death, mutilation, or general wretchedness of thousands or millions are generally rewarded with fame, riches, and prizes. The
old culture's rules speak very clearly: if you are going to rob, rob big; if
you are going to kill, kill big.

dents, functions now performed by the helicopter) and in spraying poisons on our crops.

How can we account for the lack of public resistance to this arrogance? Why does the consumer abjectly comply with every technological whim, to the point where the seller scarcely bothers to justify it, or does so with tongue in cheek? Is the man in the street so punchdrunk with technological propaganda that he can conceive of the saucer as a solution to *any* problem? How can he greet with anything but horror an invention that will blot out the sky, increase a noise level which is already intense to unbearable levels, pollute the air further, facilitate crime immeasurably, and cause hundreds of thousands of horrible accidents (translating our highway death toll to the saucer domain requires the addition of bystanders, walking about the city, sitting in their yards, sleeping in their beds, or strolling in the park) each year? Is the American public really so insane or obtuse as to relish the prospect of the sky being as filled with motorized vehicles as the ground is now?

One reason for this docility is that Americans are trained by advertising media to identify immediately with the person who actually uses the new product. When he thinks of a saucer the American imagines himself inside it, flying about and having fun. He does not think of himself trying to sleep and having other Americans roaring by his window. Nor does he think of himself trying to enjoy peace and quiet in the country with other Americans flying above. Nor does he even think of other Americans accompanying him in his flight and colliding with him as they all crowd into the city. The American in fact never thinks of other Americans at all—it is his most characteristic trait that he imagines himself to be alone on the continent.

Furthermore, Americans are always hung over from some blow dealt them by their technological environment and are always looking for a fix—for some pleasurable escape from what technology has itself created. The automobile, for example, did more than anything else to destroy community life in America. It segmented the various parts of the community and scattered them about so that they became unfamiliar with one another. It isolated travelers and decoordinated the movement of people from one place to another. It isolated and shrank living units to the point where the skills

132

involved in informal cooperation among large groups of people atrophied and were lost. As the community became a less and less satisfying and pleasurable place to be, people more and more took to their automobiles as an escape from it. This in turn crowded the roads more which generated more road-building which destroyed more communities, and so on.

The saucers will simply extend this process further. People will take to their saucers to escape the hell of a saucer-filled environment, and the more they do the more unbearable that hell will become. Each new invention is itself a refuge from the misery it creates—a new hero, a new heroin.

How far can it go? What new inventions will be offered the staggering American to help him blow up his life? Will he finally flee to outer space, leaving the nest he has so industriously fouled behind him forever? Can he really find some means to propel himself so fast that he will escape his own inventive destructiveness? Is the man in orbit—the true Nowhere Man, whirling about in his metal womb unable to encounter anyone or anything—the destiny of all Americans?

The old-culture American needs to reconsider his commitment to technological "progress." If he fails to kick the habit he may retain his culture and lose his life. One often hears old-culture adherents saying, "what will you put in its place?" ("if you don't want me to kill you, give me something else to do"). But what does a surgeon put in the place of a malignant tumor? What does a policeman put in the place of a traffic jam? What does the Food and Drug Administration put in the place of the poisoned food it confiscates? What does a society put in the place of war when peace is declared? The question assumes, first, that what exists is safe and tolerable, and second, that social systems are mere inert mechanisms with no life of their own.

Some of this resistance comes from the old culture's dependence upon the substitutes and palliatives that its own pathology necessitates. "Without all these props, wires, crutches, and pills," its adherents ask, "how can I function? Without the 'extensions of man' I am not even a person. If you take away my gas mask, how can I breathe this polluted air? How will I get to the hospital without the automobile that has made me unfit to walk?" These questions are serious, since one cannot in fact live comfortably in our society without these props until radical changes have been made—until the diseases that necessitate these palliatives have been cured. Transitions are always fraught with risk and discomfort and insecurity, but we do not enjoy the luxury of postponement. No matter how difficult it seems to engage in radical change when all is changing anyway, the risk must be taken.

Our servility toward technology, however, is no more dangerous than our exaggerated moral commitment to the "virtues" of striving and individual achievement. The mechanized disaster that surrounds us is in no small part a result of our having deluded ourselves that a motley scramble of people trying to get the better of one another is socially useful instead of something to be avoided at all costs. It has taken us a long time to realize that seeking to surpass others might be pathological, and trying to enjoy and cooperate with others healthy, rather than the other way around.

The need to triumph over each other and the tendency to prostrate ourselves before technology are in fact closely related. We turn continually to technology to save us from having to cooperate with each other. Technology, meanwhile, serves to preserve and maintain the competitive pattern and render it ever more frantic, thus making cooperation at once more urgent and more difficult.

The essentially ridiculous premises of a competitive society are masked not only by technology, but also by the complexity of our economic system and our ability to compartmentalize our thinking about it. Since we are achievement-oriented rather than satisfaction-oriented, we always think of ourselves first as producers and only second as consumers. We talk of the "beleaguered consumer" as if this referred to some specialized group of befuddled little old ladies.

To some extent this convention is a maneuver in the American war between the sexes. Since men dominate production and women consumption, the man who produces shoddy merchandise can blame his wife for being incompetent enough to purchase it for him. Men have insulated themselves to this extent from having to deal with the consequences of their behavior.

What all of our complex language about money, markets, and profits tends to mask is the fact that ultimately, when the whole circuitous process has run its course, we are producing for our own consumption. When I exploit and manipulate others, through mass media or marketing techniques, I am also exploiting and manipulating myself. The needs I generate create a treadmill that I myself will walk upon. It is true that if I manufacture shoddy goods, create artificial needs, and sell vegetables, fruit, and meat that look well but are contaminated, I will make money. But what can I do with this money? I can buy shoddy goods and poisoned food, and satisfy ersatz needs. Our refusal to recognize our common economic destiny leads to the myth that if we all overcharge each other we will be better off.

This self-delusion is even more extraordinary when we consider issues of health and safety. Why are executives living in cities indifferent to the air pollution caused by their own factories, since it is the air they and their families breathe? Or do they all live in exurbia? And what of oil company executives: have they given up ocean beaches as places of recreation? Do they all vacation at mountain lakes? Do automobile manufacturers share a secret gas mask for filtering carbon monoxide out of the air? Are the families of canning company executives immune to botulism? Those of farming tycoons immune to insecticides?

These questions are not entirely facetious. To some extent wealth does purchase immunity from the effects of the crimes perpetrated to obtain it. But in many of the examples above the effects cannot be escaped even by those who caused them. When a tanker flushes its tanks at sea or an offshore well springs a leak the oil and tar will wash up on the most exclusive beach as well as the public one. The food or drug executive cannot tell his wife not to purchase his own product, since he knows his competitors probably share the same inadequate controls. We cannot understand the irresponsibility of corporations without recognizing that it includes and *assumes* a willingness on the part of corporate leaders to endanger themselves and their families for the short-run profit of the corporation. Men have always been able to subordinate human values to the mechanisms they create. They have the capacity to invest their libido in organizations that are then viewed as having independent life and superordinate worth. Man-as-thing (producer) can then enslave man-as-person (consumer), since his narcissism is most fully bound up in his "success" as a producer. What is overlooked, of course, is that the old-culture adherent's success as a producer may bring about his death as a consumer. Furthermore, since the Nuremberg and Eichmann trials there has been a gradual but increasing reluctance to allow individuals to hide behind the fiction of corporate responsibility.

One might object at this point that the preceding discussion places so much emphasis on individual motivation that it leaves us helpless to act. We cannot expect, after all, that everyone will arise one morning resolved simultaneously to act on different premises, and thus miraculously change the society. Competitive environments are difficult to modify, since whoever takes the first step is extremely likely to go under. "The system" is certainly a reality, no matter how much it is composed of fictions.

An action program must thus consist of two parts: (1) a long-term thrust at altering motivation and (2) a short-term attempt to redirect existing institutions. As the motivational underpinnings of the society change (and they are already changing) new institutions will emerge. But so long as the old institutions maintain their present form and thrust they will tend to overpower and corrupt the new ones. During the transitional period, then, those who seek peaceful and gradual change should work toward liberal reforms that shift the incentive *structure* as motivations in fact change.

Imagine that we are all inhabitants of a large and inescapable boat, marooned in a once ample but now rapidly shrinking lake. For generations we have been preoccupied with finding ways to make the boat sail faster around the lake. But now we find we have been all too successful, for the lake gets smaller and smaller and the boat goes faster and faster. Some people are saying that since the lake is about to disappear we must develop a new way of life, that is to say, learn to live on land. They say that in any case going in circles on a little lake is an absurd way of life. Others cling to the old ways and say that living on land is immoral. There is also a middle-of-the-road group that says living on the lake is best but perhaps we had better slow down before we smash to pieces on the ever-nearer rocks around and below us.

Now if it is true that the lake is disappearing, those who want to live on land must not only prepare themselves and convert others, but must also train the captain and crew to navigate on land. And the middle-of-the-roaders must not only try to find ways to slow the boat down, but should also seek some way to attach wheels to its bottom. Putting wheels on the boat is what I mean by liberal reform of the incentive structure. It is a technique of softening the impact of the collision between old and new.

Let me give a concrete example of adjusting institutions to match motivational changes. It seems quite clear that a far smaller proportion of college graduates today are interested in careers of personal aggrandizement, compared with twenty years ago. Far more want to devote themselves to social problems of one kind and another, or to helping individuals who are disadvantaged in some way. This is surely a beneficial shift in emphasis—we perhaps do not need as many people as we once did to enrich themselves at our expense, and we have no place to put the overpriced junk we already have. But our old-culture institutions continually place obstacles in the path of this shift. Those who seek to provide services are often prevented by established members of the professions—such as doctors, teachers, and social workers—since the principle behind any professional organization is (a) to restrict membership and (b) to provide minimum service at maximum cost. Draft boards also discriminate against this kind of social altruism, and law enforcement agencies often punish it.

The most interesting form of discrimination is that of the Internal Revenue Service. The whole complex fabric of income tax regulations rests on the principle of rewarding single-minded devotion to self-aggrandizement (the deduction for contributions is a trivial exception to this rule). If one spent all his money protecting, maintaining, or trying to increase his income he would theoretically pay no tax whatever. The tax structure rewards the moneygrubber, the wheeler-dealer, and punishes the man who simply provides a service and is paid something for it. The man who devotes his life to making money is rewarded by the United States Government with tax loopholes, while the man who devotes his life to service picks up the check.

We need to reverse these incentives. We need to reward everyone *except* the money-hungry—to reward those who are helping others rather than themselves. Actually, this could be done very easily by simply eliminating the entire absurd structure of deductions, exemptions, and allowances, and thus taxing the rich and avaricious instead of the poor and altruistic. This would have other advantages as well: discouraging overpopulation and home ownership, and saving millions of man-hours of senseless and unrewarding clerical labor.

Reforms in the kinds of priorities involved in the disbursement of federal funds would also help. At present, almost 80 percent of the federal budget is devoted to life-destroying activities, only about 10 percent to life-enhancing ones. The ending of the war should be the first item on everyone's agenda, but even without the war there is much to be done in the way of priority changes. At present most government spending subsidizes the rich: defense spending subsidizes war contractors, foreign aid subsidizes exporters, the farm program subsidizes rich farmers, highway and urban redevelopment programs subsidize building contractors, medical programs subsidize doctors and drug companies, and so on. Some programs, like the poverty program, subsidize middle-class service-oriented people to some extent, and this is helpful. It is probably impossible to subsidize the poor themselves with existing techniques—such a profound reversal of pattern requires a more radical approach, like the negative income tax or guaranteed employment.

It must be made clear that we are not trying to make money-grubbers out of those who are not, but rather to restore money to its rightful place as a medium of exchange—to reduce the role of money as an instrument of vanity. Under present conditions those with the greatest need for narcissistic self-aggrandizement can amass enormous unused surpluses, and this process the Government tends to reward and encourage. The shortages thereby created tend to make it difficult for middle-class people who are less interested in self-aggrandizement to maintain their secular attitude toward money. The poorer working class and the destitute, meanwhile, are thrown into such an acute state of deprivation that money comes to overshadow other goals. Since we know from long experience with children of the affluent that familiarity with money tends to breed contempt, whatever we can do to equalize the distribution of wealth will tend to create disinterest. This will leave only the most pathological narcissists still money-oriented—indeed, they will be worse than ever, since they will have been deprived of their surplus millions or of the opportunity of amassing them, and will have to look elsewhere for the means of gratifying their vanity. Perhaps they will seek it through the exercise of power—becoming generals or teachers or doctors; perhaps through fame, becoming writers or artists or scholars. In any case, money would tend to be sought by the ordinary person merely to obtain specific goods or services.

Such a profound transformation is not likely to occur soon. Yet it is interesting that it is precisely the reversal of the incentive structure that is most feared by critics of such plans as the negative income tax. Why would people want to work and strive, they ask, if they could get all they wanted to eat without it? Why would they be willing to sell out their friends, sacrifice family ties, cheat and swindle themselves and everyone else, and disregard social problems and needs, if in fact they could obtain goods and services without doing these things? "They would have to be sick," we hear someone say, and this is the correct answer. Only the sick would do it—those who today when they have a million dollars keep striving for more. *But the non-sick would be free from the obligation to behave as if they were sick—an obligation our society presently enjoins.* It would not be made so difficult, if these proposals were carried out, for Americans to be motivated by something other than greed. People engaged in helping others, in making communities viable, in making the environment more attractive, would be able to live more comfortably if they wished. Some people would of course do nothing at all but amuse themselves, like the idle rich, and this seems to disturb people: "subsidized idleness," they call it, as if thus to discredit it. Yet I personally would far rather pay people *not* to make nerve gas than pay them to make it; pay them *not* to pollute the environment than pay them to do it; pay them *not* to inundate us with instant junk than pay them to do it; pay them *not* to swindle us than pay them to do it; pay them *not* to kill peasants than pay them to do it; pay them *not* to be dictators than pay them to do it; pay them *not* to replace communities with highways than pay them to do it, and so on. One thing must be said for idleness: it keeps people from doing the Devil's work. The great villains of history were busy men, since great crimes and slaughters require great industry and dedication.

Those skilled in social and political action can probably devise many more profound programs for defusing the perverse incentive structure our society now enjoys, but the foregoing will at least serve to exemplify the point I wish to make. As a general rule it can be said that every institution, every program in our society should be examined to determine whether it encourages social consciousness or personal aggrandizement.

Let us now turn to the question of long-range modifications in motivation. For no matter how much we try to eliminate scarcity assumptions from the incentive structures of our institutions, they will continue to reemerge if we do not devote some attention to reforming the psychic structures that our family patterns generate in children.

Some people may feel that this is already happening. The new culture has burgeoned among the younger generation, after all, and the new culture is founded on a rejection of scarcity assumptions. The "sexual revolution" promises to eliminate altogether the libidinal foundation for scarcity psychology. Furthermore, this liberalization of sexual norms is predictably leading to a more generalized movement toward the liberation of women (predictably because historically, sexual restrictions have been imposed primarily on women). Mothers of the future should therefore be far less inclined than in the past to flood their male children with frustrated longings and resentments. Living fuller and less constricted lives themselves they should have less need to invest their children with Oedipally tinged ambition.

I am nonetheless skeptical that this will occur in the absence of other changes—changes which will not come from, but must be learned by, the young. The problem arises at the point at which new-culture adherents enter the sphere now dominated by the old culture. This sphere has three portals: graduation, marriage, and parenthood—each one a more powerful instrument of old-culture seduction than the last. Indeed, old-culture adherents count heavily on this triple threat to force youthful "idealists" to relinquish their commitment to change. There is a gloating quality to their expectancy ("wait until they have to raise a family"), which turns rather ugly when it is disappointed ("You gotta grow up *sometime*").

These expectations are often confirmed—not because there is anything inherently mature or adult about living in a suburb or cheating your neighbor, but because the new culture has made few inroads into the structure of post-college life. New-culture students are leaving an environment in which their attitudes are widely shared and moving into one in which they will be isolated, surrounded, and shunted onto a series of conveyor belts that carry one into the old culture with a certain inevitable logic that can be resisted only with deliberate and perpetual effort.

Students know this and fear it. They dread becoming like their parents but cannot see how to avoid it. It is as if they had come to the edge of a dense, overgrown forest, penetrable only by a series of smooth, easily traversed paths, all of which, however, have signs saying "To the Quicksand."

Graduation always looks like the most dangerous seduction, but in fact it is the least. With great struggles, floundering, and anxiety, students are managing increasingly to carve out lives for themselves that do not commit them fully to the old culture. Some compromise by going to graduate school, which is more dangerous, since all professions have subtle initiation rites built into their training procedures, based on the it-must-have-been-worth-it-or-I-wouldn't-have-done-it principle. But even here some new-culture adherents have been able to hold their own, and every profession has sprouted a small but indestructible new-culture wing.

Fear of marriage and of bad marital relationships is almost as strong, but seems not to be a deterrent. Students marry in droves anyway, perhaps to obtain security for their resistance to occupational seduction. Parenthood is least feared of all, although it is clearly the most dangerous, for it was parenthood that played the largest part in the corruption of their own parents. "For the children" is second only to "for God and country" as a rallying cry for public atrocities. The new parents will undoubtedly interpret the slogan in somewhat less materialistic terms, but the old culture and the new share the same child-oriented attitude. This creates many pitfalls for unwary neophyte parents, since the old culture has a built-in system of automatic, escalating choice-points to translate this attitude into old-culture practices. The minute the parents decide they want their child to have some green grass to run about in, or a school that is not taught by rigid, authoritarian teachers, they will suddenly discover that they have eaten a piece of the gingerbread house and are no longer free.

Even in this case, of course, there are solutions, just as in the occupational sphere. But less thought and attention have been given to this problem by the young. They imagine, like every fool who ever had children, that their own experiences as children will guide them and protect them against their own parents' errors. People in our society are particularly blind to the overwhelming force of role identification, and they are also peculiarly unprepared, by the insulation of their youth culture, for its sudden onset. In more traditional cultures everyone realizes that upon becoming parents they will tend automatically to mimic their own parents' behavior, but in our society this comes as a shock, and is often not even perceived.

To this must be added still another powerful factor—peculiar in its intensity, perhaps, to this generation. The parents of today's youth tended to sacrifice much of their own pleasure to the manufacturing of successful children. Much comment has been made to the effect that student protest represents a continuing expectation of adult self-sacrifice. Perhaps so, but I am even more impressed by the diffuse sense of guilt and responsibility that afflicts contemporary students. I suspect strongly that the advent of parenthood will provide a highly seductive vehicle for expression of these feelings, especially since the new culture is highly pro-child anyway, and hence provides no warning signs. Many will find not only that they have boarded the old-culture's child-oriented suburban family conveyor belt, but that the timely provision of this opportunity for the release of parent-induced feelings of guilt and responsibility will drain off much of their social concern.

It is difficult, in other words, not to repeat patterns that are as deeply rooted in primary emotional experiences as these are, particularly when one is unprepared. The new parents may not be as absorbed in material possessions and occupational self-aggrandizement as their own parents were. They may channel their parental vanity into different spheres, pushing their children to be brilliant artists, thinkers, and performers. But the hard narcissistic core on which the old culture was based will not be dissolved until the parent-child relationship itself is de-intensified, and this is precisely where the younger generation is likely to be most inadequate. While the main body of the cell of the old culture is being constantly weakened, its nucleus is in danger of being transferred, not only intact, but strengthened—like a bacterial strain resistant to drugs—to the new.

It is not that being child-oriented itself produces a narcissistic personality—quite the contrary. It is when the parent turns to the child as a vicarious substitute for satisfactions the parent fails to find in his or her own life that the child becomes vain, ambitious, hungry for glory. Both the likelihood and the intensity of this pattern are increased when the family is a small, nuclear, isolated unit and the child socialized by few other adults. Our society has from the beginning, and increasingly with each generation, tended to foster "Oedipal" children. New-culture adherents want desperately to build a cooperative, communal world, but they are in some ways the least likely people in the world to be able to do it, or to produce children that could do it. They cannot break the Oedipal pattern alone because they are even more enmeshed in it than were their parents.

Breaking the pattern means establishing communities in which (a) children are not socialized exclusively by their parents, (b) parents have lives of their own and do not live vicariously through their children, hence (c) life is lived for the present, not the future, and hence (d) middle-aged and elderly people participate in the community in the same way as youth and vice versa. This constellation of traits forms a coherent unit, as does its opposite.

Although the reasons are obvious, it is ironic that young people who try to form communes almost always create the same narrow, age-graded, class homogeneous society in which they were formed. This is in part because they know few older or working-class adults who might conceivably participate. But in part it reflects the same future-oriented psychology that produced the old-culture family system they are trying to supersede. Again we are confronted with the paradox of trying to build a future that does not always look to the future. We need desperately a social change mechanism that is self-extinguishing. Revolutionary ideologies always *assume* that change and fascination with the future will cease once the golden day arrives, but they never include any means even for slowing it down.

Older adults have a vested interest in finding a place for themselves in the new society, and whatever place they find will provide a model for new-culture adherents as they age. In the old culture there is no place at all for the aged, and old-culture adherents are growing older. They have the option of sitting back and enjoying the fact that ultimately their misery will be shared by those who follow, or of working toward a reversal of the pattern—a reversal that will profit posterity somewhat more than themselves. Their presence will help to dilute the future-orientation that new-culture adherents must of necessity have. Without this—without an attempt to establish bridges and continuities and balances, to understand where the present connects with and remodels past trends (for only the combinations and arrangements change, the elements are deathless)—the society they build will have the same defects as the old one. The old culture attempts ruthlessly to cut the past away, and thereby digs itself deeper into a morass of meaninglessness and chaos. What the new culture seeks is wholeness, and obviously it cannot achieve this by exclusion. A community that does not have old people and children, white-collar and blue-collar, eccentric and conventional, and so on, is not a community at all, but the same kind of truncated and deformed monstrosity that most people inhabit today.

What I have been saying may sound excessively utopian even to those adults who feel drawn to the new culture. Can any middle-aged person, trained as he is in the role considered appropriate to his age, find anything in the new culture to which he can attach himself without feeling absurd? Can he "act his age" in the new culture? There are indeed severe contradictions between the two, but syntheses are also to be found. Adults in encounter groups usually discover that much of what is new-culture is not at all alien or uncomfortable for them. There are many roles that can and must be carved out for older people, for otherwise we will still have the same kind of ice-floe approach to the aged that we now have.

HAZARDS OF UNPLANNED CHANGE

Americans have always entertained the strange fantasy that change can occur easily and without pain. This pleasant idea springs from a confusion between change (the alteration of behavior patterns) and novelty (the rotation of stimuli within a pattern). Americans talk about social change as if it involved nothing more than re-arranging the contents of a display window. But real change is difficult and painful, which perhaps explains why Americans have abandoned all responsibility for initiating it to technology and the rotation of generations.

Given general recognition by old-culture adherents of the necessity for change, and equally general commitment to it, there is no particular reason why the United States could not become the center of the most beautiful, benign, and exciting culture the world has ever known. We have always been big, and have done things in big ways; having lately become in many ways the worst of societies we could just as easily become the best. No society, after all, has ever solved the problems that now confront us. Potentiality has always been our most attractive characteristic, which is one reason why we have always been so reluctant to commit ourselves to finally realizing it. But perhaps the time has come to make that commitment—to abandon our adolescent dreams of omnipotentiality and demonstrate that we actually *can* create a palatable society. America is like a student who is proud of having somehow survived without serious work, and likes to imagine that if he really put any effort into it he could achieve everything, but is unwilling to endanger so lovely a dream by making an actual commitment to anything.

Unfortunately, while young activists have developed a variety of innovative and successful strategies that are revolutionary in their impact, they have as yet been unable to integrate these around a truly modern theory of revolutionary change, attaching them instead to a horse-and-buggy political theory onto which has been grafted, with prodigious pedantic effort, an outboard motor and some bicycle tires. Their achievements already deserve better than this. They have used media brilliantly, for example, yet operate with a theory that takes very inadequate account of this.

The fundamental political goal of the new culture is the diffusion of power, just as its fundamental economic goal is the diffusion of wealth. Marxist theory seeks to achieve this through a transfer of concentrated power into the hands of revolutionaries, in order first to secure economic diffusion. In the United States, however, economic diffusion is a far more easily attained goal than the diffusion of power, so that it becomes more important to ensure the latter, and to be skeptical of its postponement.

Activists have achieved considerable dispersion of power on a local scale merely through unmasking, exposing, and threatening to expose those at the centers of power. The ability to maintain a permanent concentration of power depends upon the ability to maintain and enforce secrecy, and dispersal tends to follow automatically upon breakdown of this ability. Old-culture leaders are peculiarly vulnerable on this point because they are not sensitive to certain inherent characteristics of mass media. They think in terms of news management and press releases and public statements—of *controlling* the media in the old-fashioned propagandistic sense. Indeed, traditional Marxists share their views, and devote their energies to worrying about the fact that all news media are controlled by a relatively small number of wealthy and conservative men. New-culture activists, on the other hand, are attuned to the media. They recognize that the media are *inherently* stimulus-hungry, and that by their very nature they seek exposure and drama. They know a crowd is more interesting than a press conference, a march than a speech. Successful use of television today requires an improvisational looseness and informality that old-culture leaders lack. Their carefully managed statements become too obviously hollow with repetition, their pomposity too easily punctured by an awkward incident, their lies too recently stated and well-remembered to be ignored. It seems astonishing to us when statesmen and generals who support the war in Vietnam put themselves in the position of saying, in effect, "Well, I lied to you before, but this time I'm telling the truth." But prior to television it was quite possible to assume that the mass of the population was substantially without memory.

I am suggesting that with increasing numbers, and the expansion of the arena of protest and confrontation, the diffusion of power could occur with little change in the *formal* machinery of government, which, after all, can lend itself to a wide range of political types. Instead of a single traditional revolution, concentrated in time and space (the notion of a crowd descending on the White House with carbines seems hopelessly archaic), one can imagine a prolonged series of revolutionary challenges occurring in one segment of the society after another, forcing dispersion of power in every kind of organizational structure.

But if old-culture adherents ignore or resist the process of transition there is a strong danger that this decentralized revolution will be countered by a centralized coup from the right. There are a number of factors that make this danger real and immediate. First, those elements in our society with the strongest commitment to military pursuits and old-culture principles have a virtual monopoly on the more powerful and ingenious weapons in our Gargantuan arsenal. The mere threat to release nerve gas in a troublesome area, for example, would have an extremely repressive impact on the population involved. Second, these same groups—the Pentagon, the CIA, the FBI and other law enforcement agencies—share the highest secrecy quotient allowed in the nation. They are very largely protected from scrutiny and can operate in undercover ways impossible for any other segment of government. Third, they include the only agencies equipped to ferret out and expose such a plot, yet they themselves are heavily populated by people highly motivated to participate in it. Fourth, their task is facilitated by the fact that the machinery now exists, under present laws, for placing in concentration camps every left or liberal leader in the country. The camps exist, as do the files, and the procedures to be adopted. Should military groups ever decide to shrug off civilian control a single order is all that would be required to eliminate all active opposition to right-wing sentiment.

The likelihood of this happening increases daily, as the clash between the two cultures accelerates. The transition, after all, has only begun, yet already people are frightened by the few confrontations that have taken place. Disruption and paralysis are going to increase during the transition unless efforts are made to ease the process, and many old-culture adherents will provide popular support for anyone who promises, like Hitler, to restore law and order.

Most Americans still just want to go about their business and ignore the problems of their society, and are willing to pay a very heavy price to be able to do so.

Such a coup might well be combined with a right-induced nuclear war. Controls to prevent such an "accident" are extremely inadequate, as several ill-reported near-disasters have shown; when the old culture falls it may take the entire world with it. Furthermore, as the technological blight of our society continues, it seems to many less and less worth preserving. It then becomes futile to argue self-preservation against nuclear hawks—more and more people feel with a larger and larger part of themselves that the destruction of mankind as a failed species might be a sound idea.

It thus becomes urgent for moderates not only to facilitate the retooling of our society from killing and competing to cooperating and enjoying, but also to detach power from those who hate life and would rather die themselves than see others enjoying it. But this raises an awkward dilemma: in a satisfying society who else would want power? What but a kind of sickness would drive people to attain such power over others? Would not the sickest people wind up with the most power, even more regularly than they do now? If power is diffused, on the other hand, will not the entire population be corrupted by this sickness?

The answer to this last question is No. Nothing is poisonous if taken in small enough quantities, and the more power is diffused the more the assumption of power looks like the assumption of responsibility. It is when power is concentrated that the pursuit of it takes on an unhealthy hue. It is perhaps one of the best arguments for participatory democracy that the alternative to participation in the drudgery of government is being governed by the sick and perverse.

I can best summarize my various predictive comments by saying that old-culture moderates or liberals will be given the choice, during the next decade or so, between participating in some way in the new culture and living under a fascist regime. The middle is dropping out of things and choices must be made. If the old culture is rejected, the new must be ushered in as gracefully as possible. If the old culture is not rejected then its adherents must be prepared to accept a bloodbath such as has not been seen in the United States since the Civil War, for genocidal weapons will be on one side and unarmed masses on the other.

The best key to the kind of future we can expect is the university —the first victim of the clash between the two cultures. The university is a remarkably vulnerable institution, since it lies directly in the path of the rapidly swelling ranks of the new culture yet bears a poorly concealed parasitic relation to the old. It is thus caught in a vise—it cannot ignore the new culture as the rest of society attempts to do, yet it cannot accommodate to it without losing old-culture support and going bankrupt. No solutions will be found to this dilemma until some of the institutions on which the university depends begin to yield and change, and many universities will go under before this happens. If the universities—notoriously rigid and archaic institutions—can find ways to absorb the new culture this augurs well for the society as a whole. If, on the other hand, the campus becomes a police state, as many are suggesting, it seems likely that the nation as a whole will follow the same path.

ALONE TOGETHER

The most serious internal danger to the new culture is the insidious transmission of individualism from the old culture, in part through confusion with the new culture's otherwise healthy emphasis on emotional expression. Ambivalence about the issue of individualism-versus-social-commitment is deep and unresolved. On the one hand there is increasing experimentation with communes and communal arrangements, and a serious awareness of the Nuremberg Trials and their proclamation of man's personal responsibility to all men. On the other hand there is great fascination with the concept of anarchy—with the attempt to eliminate coercion and commitment in any form from human life.

But to generalize the need to free oneself from the emotional barrenness and depersonalized control mechanisms of the old culture to freedom from *all* social conditions is simply to return the new culture to the old one. Anarchy is merely a radical extension of the old culture. It is also a way of retaining the pristine American fantasy of being special—a condition which American society promises, and withholds, more than any society in history. The unstated rider to "do your own thing" is that everybody will watch —that a special superiority will be granted and acknowledged by others.* But in a satisfying society this specialness is not needed, and for a satisfying society to exist the recognition that people can and must make demands upon one another must also exist. Any community worthy of the name (one in which the relationships between people are regulated by people, instead of by machines) would seem "totalitarian" to today's youth, not in the sense of having an authoritarian leadership structure, but in the sense of permitting group intrusion into what is for most Americans the private sphere. This will be the most difficult problem new-culture adherents will face, for we are long accustomed to an illusory freedom based on subtle compulsion by technology and bureaucratic mechanisms. But there is no way for large numbers of people to coexist without governing and being governed by each other, unless they establish machines to do it; at which point they risk losing sight and understanding of the interconnectedness itself—a process well advanced in our culture today. There is something wildly comic about cars stopping and starting in response to a traffic light, for example, but most Americans have lost the capacity to experience it. It seems right and natural for machines to tell us how to relate to each other.

The goal of many early Americans was to find or to create or to participate in a utopian community, but they became distracted by the dream of personal aggrandizement and found themselves farther and farther from this goal. When we think today of the kind of social compliance that exists in such communities (as well as in the primitive communities we romanticize so much) we shrink in horror. We tell each other chilling stories of individuals in imagined societies of the future being forced to give up their dreams for the good of the group, of not being allowed to stand out. But this, in

---

* I recognize, of course, that there are positive aspects to individualism, that even if it were possible to eliminate it altogether it would probably not be desirable. There is a pleasurable tension in romanticism and the heroic myth, and communal, un-Oedipal children tend to be a little literal and uninteresting. An exaggerated swing of the pendulum in this direction, however, is not a problem we will have to worry about in *this* century.

some degree, is just the price we must pay for a tolerable life in a tolerable community. We need to understand this price, to consider it, to reflect on its consequences and the consequences of not paying it. Is an occasional group viciousness really worse than the unfocused universal snarl that has replaced it in our mechanically regulated society? It is the structured narcissism of the old culture that brings down upon our heads all of the evils we detest, and we will only escape these evils when we have abandoned the narcissistic dreams that sustain them.

Past efforts to build utopian communities failed because they were founded on scarcity assumptions. But scarcity is now shown to be an unnecessary condition, and the distractions that it generated can now be avoided. We need not raise the youth of new utopias to feel that life's primary gratifications are in such short supply. Hence the only obstacle to utopia is the persistence of the competitive motivational patterns that past scarcity assumptions have spawned. Nothing stands in our way except our invidious dreams of personal glory. Our horror of group coercion reflects our reluctance to relinquish these dreams, although they have brought us nothing but misery, discontent, hatred, and chaos. If we can overcome this horror, however, and mute this vanity, we may again be able to take up our original utopian task.

Notes

CHAPTER 1

1. S. A. Stouffer, *Communism, Conformity, and Civil Liberties* (New York: Wiley, 1966), p. 164. Italics mine.

2. Ezra F. Vogel and Suzanne H. Vogel, "Permissive Dependency in Japan," in H. Kent Geiger (ed.), *Comparative Perspectives on Marriage and the Family* (Boston: Little, Brown, 1968), pp. 68–77.

3. See Erich Fromm, *Escape from Freedom* (New York: Rinehart, 1941); W. G. Bennis and P. E. Slater, *The Temporary Society* (New York: Harper and Row, 1968), Chapter 1. Bennis and I attempt to show that the "efficiency" Americans attribute to autocratic systems applies only to situations involving simple, routine tasks. Such systems function poorly under conditions of change and complexity. They have an awkward tendency to run a "tight ship" which nevertheless sinks.

4. S. H. King and A. F. Henry, "Aggression and Cardiovascular Reactions Related to Parental Control over Behavior," *Journal of Abnormal and Social Psychology*, LIII, 1955, pp. 206–210.

5. David Riesman, *Individualism Reconsidered* (Garden City, New York: Doubleday Anchor, 1954), p. 27. This is a principle for which nature has shown a fine disregard—evolution proceeds on a diametrically opposite principle.

6. Jay Haley, "The Family of the Schizophrenic: A Model System," in G. Handel (ed.), *The Psychosocial Interior of the Family* (Chicago: Aldine, 1967), pp. 271–272.

CHAPTER 2

1. Frank Harvey, *Air War—Vietnam* (New York: Bantam, 1967); Robert Crichton, "Our Air War," *New York Review of Books*, IX, January 4, 1968.

2. Harvey, pp. 15, 29–30, 67, 100, 104, 108–109, 115.

3. Harvey, pp. 2, 16, 55–56, 107, 116.

4. Harvey, pp. 108, 141, 146–147, 150, 154; Crichton, p. 3.

5. Harvey, pp. 54–57, 82 ff.; Crichton, pp. 3–4.

6. Harvey, pp. 57, 91–92, 102–104, 115, 174–175; Crichton, pp. 3–4.

7. Harvey, pp. 39–40, 62–63, 106–107, 126–127; Crichton, p. 4.

8. Harvey, pp. 65, 70, 72, 105, 109, 111, 112, 138, 150, 152; Crichton, pp. 3–4.

9. Harvey, pp. 5–8, 11, 63, 115.

10. Bennis and Slater, *The Temporary Society*, Chapter 2.

11. Martha Wolfenstein and Nathan Leites, *Movies: A Psychological Study* (Glencoe, Ill.: Free Press, 1950), pp. 106 ff., 149–174.

12. Margaret Mead, *Sex and Temperament in Three Primitive Societies* (New York: Mentor, 1950), p. 21.

CHAPTER 3

1. Donald Barthelme, *Snow White* (New York: Bantam, 1968), p. 131.

2. Paul Potter, quoted by Warren G. Bennis in "Future of the Social Sciences," *Antioch Review*, XXVIII, Summer 1968, p. 239.

3. Theodore Lidz, et al., *Schizophrenia and the Family* (New York: International Universities Press, 1965), p. 182.

4. See Bennis and Slater, *The Temporary Society*, Chapter 2.

5. John L. Fischer and Ann Fischer, "The New Englanders of Orchard Town, U.S.A.," in Beatrice Whiting (ed.), *Six Cultures: Studies of Child Rearing* (New York: Wiley, 1963), pp. 921–928.

6. Benjamin Spock, *Baby and Child Care* (New York: Pocket Books, 1968), p. 12. See also pp. xvi, 10–23.

7. Ibid., pp. 563–564.

8. P. E. Slater, *The Glory of Hera* (Boston: Beacon Press, 1968), pp. 450–451; see also *The Temporary Society*, pp. 91–92.

9. I am indebted to Dori Appel Slater for this observation.

10. The Glory of Hera, Chapters 1, 14, 15. See also Beatrice Whiting, "Sex Identity Conflict and Physical Violence: A Comparative Study," *American Anthropologist*, LXVII, December 1965 Supplement, pp. 123–140; R. V. Burton and J. W. M. Whiting, "The Absent Father and Cross-Sex Identity," *Merrill-Palmer Quarterly*, VII, 1961, pp. 85–95.

11. Eldridge Cleaver, *Soul on Ice* (New York: McGraw-Hill, 1968), pp. 191–204.

12. William H. Whyte, Jr., "The Wife Problem," in R. F. Winch, et al. (eds.), *Selected Studies in Marriage and the Family* (New York: Holt, Rinehart, and Winston, 1962), pp. 472–477.

13. See Melvin L. Kohn, "Social Class and Parental Values," *American Journal of Sociology*, LXIV, 1959, pp. 337–351, for a study of the different child-rearing aspirations of middle-class and working-class families. The latter seek obedience, neatness, and cleanliness, while middle-class parents seem to take these for granted and seek internal qualities such as curiosity, self-control, and happiness.

14. Thomas Cottle, "Parent and Child—The Hazards of Equality," *Saturday Review*, February 1, 1969, pp. 16 ff.

CHAPTER 4

1. R. Lynn, "Anxiety and Economic Growth," in *Nature*, 219, 1968, pp. 765–766.

2. S. Freud, *Civilization and Its Discontents* (London: Hogarth, 1953), pp. 74, 92, 142–143.

3. J. D. Unwin, *Sex and Culture* (London: Oxford, 1934); G. P. Murdock, "The Regulation of Premarital Sex Behavior," in R. A. Manners (ed.), *Process and Pattern in Culture* (Chicago: Aldine, 1964), 399–410; P. E. Slater, "Culture, Sexuality, and Narcissism: A Cross-Cultural Study" (unpublished paper, 1965). See also H. Marcuse, *Eros and Civilization* (Boston: Beacon Press, 1955); N. O. Brown, *Life Against Death* (New York: Vintage, 1959).

4. P. E. Slater, "Some Social Psychological Characteristics of Warlike Cultures" (unpublished paper, 1966); J. Dollard, et al., *Frustration and Aggression* (New Haven: Yale University Press, 1939); Grace Stuart, *Narcissus* (New York: Macmillan, 1955).

5. Fred Cottrell, *Energy and Society* (New York: McGraw-Hill, 1955), p. 4.

6. A. R. Holmberg, *Nomads of the Long Bow* (Washington: U.S. Government Printing Office, 1950).

7. For a discussion of the ways in which a particularly extreme form of sexual scarcity may have begun, see *The Glory of Hera*, Chapters 1 and 15. Freud's primal horde myth might be viewed as a description of the diffusion of sexual scarcity: a sexually monopolistic despot (or conquering tribe) deprives weaker males of sexual access to women. They, rendered unquiet by this, become increasingly prone to revolt, eventually do so (perhaps by inventing a new weapon), but retain some sexual restrictions—not out of guilt, but from some vague recognition that to such restrictions they owe their victory.

For a well-supported theory of the origin of the postpartum sex taboo in dietary and birth control needs, see J. W. M. Whiting, "Effects of Climate on Certain Cultural Practices," in W. H. Goodenough (ed.), *Exploration in Cultural Anthropology* (New York: McGraw-Hill, 1964), pp. 511–544.

8. Cf., e.g., W. N. Stephens, *The Oedipus Complex* (Glencoe, Ill.: Free Press, 1962).

9. Cf., e.g., C. S. Ford and F. A. Beach, *Patterns of Sexual Behavior* (New York: Harper, 1951), p. 78.

10. Cf. Denis de Rougemont, *Love in the Western World* (Garden City, New York: Doubleday Anchor, 1957); J. C. Flugel, *The Psycho-analytic Study of the Family* (London: Hogarth, 1957); S. Freud, *Collected Papers*, Vol. IV (London: Hogarth, 1953), pp. 192–216; R. Kastenbaum (ed.), *New Thoughts on Old Age* (New York: Springer, 1964), pp. 19–40.

11. See Slater, "Some Social Psychological Characteristics of Warlike Cultures." Cf. also Stuart, *Narcissus.*

12. Erving Goffman, *Behavior in Public Places* (New York: Free Press, 1963), pp. 56–59.

13. Soul on Ice, pp. 202–203.

CHAPTER 5

1. Herbert Marcuse, *An Essay on Liberation* (Boston: Beacon Press, 1969), pp. 66, 73, 77–78.

2. Lewis Mumford, "The Fallacy of Systems," *Saturday Review of Literature,* XXXII, October 1949; Gideon Sjoberg, "Contradictory Functional Requirements of Social Systems," *Journal of Conflict Resolution,* IV, 1960, pp. 198–208.

3. See, for example, Robert Houriet, "Life and Death of a Commune Called Oz," *New York Times Magazine,* February 16, 1969.

4. Leon Festinger, *A Theory of Cognitive Dissonance* (Stanford, Calif.: Stanford University Press, 1965).

CHAPTER 6

1. Herbert Marcuse, *An Essay on Liberation* (Boston: Beacon Press, 1969), p. 18. As humanists so often do, Marcuse tries to devise a conceptual system in which all the things one likes fall into one category and all those things one dislikes into another. But "good" and "bad" are always orthogonal to important distinctions.

2. S. Freud, *Civilization and Its Discontents* (London: Hogarth, 1953), pp. 46–48. One could also make this argument for art: if our emotional life were not so impoverished by the sacrifices we make to utility, we would not need art to enrich it. See *The Glory of Hera,* pp. 463–464.

3. Alvin Smith, *Boston Sunday Globe,* January 5, 1969.

DATE DUE

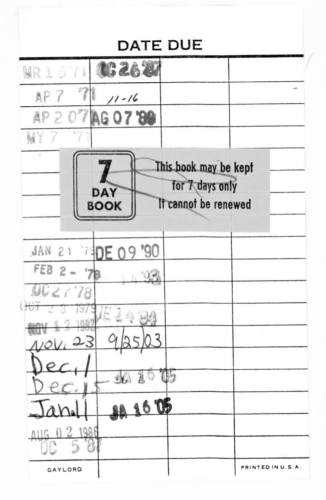

MR 15 '71	OC 26 '87		
AP 7 '71	11-16		
AP 2 0 '7	AG 07 '89		
MY 7 '7			
JAN 21 '7	DE 09 '90		
FEB 2 - '78			
OC 2 '78			
OCT 2 3 1979	JE 14 '94		
NOV 1 2 1982			
NOV. 23	9/25/03		
Dec.1			
Dec.15	JA 16 05		
Jan.11	JA 16 05		
AUG 0 2 1986			
OC 5 8			